T0358459

*Routledge Revivals*

# The Conditions of Industrial Peace

First published in 1927, Hobson's treatise on industrial conflict analyses the nature and causes of industrial disputes with the aim of finding an equitable means of settling them. Assessing the notion of a fair wage within the context of the pool of wealth, Hobson sets about creating a peace policy for industry. Set against the backdrop of economic downturn and struggle in the interwar years, in the years preceding the great depression, this is a work of social, historical and economic interest.

# The Conditions of Industrial Peace

## J. A. Hobson

Routledge
Taylor & Francis Group

First published in 1927
by George Allen & Unwin Ltd

This edition first published in 2012 by Routledge
2 Park Square, Milton Park, Abingdon, Oxon, OX14 4RN

Simultaneously published in the USA and Canada
by Routledge
711 Third Avenue, New York, NY 10017

*Routledge is an imprint of the Taylor & Francis Group, an informa business*

**Publisher's Note**
The publisher has gone to great lengths to ensure the quality of this
reprint but points out that some imperfections in the original copies may
be apparent.

**Disclaimer**
The publisher has made every effort to trace copyright holders and
welcomes correspondence from those they have been unable to contact.

A Library of Congress record exists under LC Control Number: 1
27000306


ISBN 13: 978-0-415-52538-1 (hbk)
ISBN 13: 978-0-203-11846-7 (ebk)

# THE CONDITIONS OF
# INDUSTRIAL PEACE

# THE CONDITIONS OF
# INDUSTRIAL PEACE

BY

## J. A. HOBSON

LONDON : GEORGE ALLEN & UNWIN LTD.
RUSKIN HOUSE, 40 MUSEUM STREET, W.C. 1

*First published in 1927*
*(All rights reserved)*

*Printed in Great Britain by*
*Unwin Brothers, Ltd., Woking*

# PREFACE

IT is generally recognised that industrial conflicts issuing in strikes and lockouts, with their waste, disorder, misery and malice, can only be averted by the willing consent of the parties to submit their differences for settlement to some equitable and impartial tribunal. It seems so evidently just and reasonable that disputants should not be judges in their own cause and administer by economic force their self-made justice, as to blind many minds to the difficulties that beset this path of reason. Most trade disputes relate to the terms upon which workers will undertake employment, the price of labour. Even when hours or other conditions figure in the front of a dispute, they mean to the employer 'cost of production.' Now all business is so permeated by the notion that prices shall be fixed by the relative strength of bargaining between sellers and buyers, and that every seller and buyer has full liberty to refuse to sell or buy, if he does not find the price acceptable, that business men, whether employers or workers, experience a shock when it is suggested that the sale of labour must be conducted in some other way, if industry is to function successfully. Yet this is the meaning of the demand that grave trade disputes shall be submitted to arbitration, with some legal or moral compulsion to accept the award. It seems an encroachment upon personal liberty.

If this feeling is to be overcome, the whole problem of industrial peace must be envisaged in its broader setting, and preliminary measures must be taken for limiting the areas of conflict.   In the first place, the crucial fact that the economic consequences of a trade dispute cannot be confined to the disputants in the particular trade, but must always extend with varying degrees of intensity to other trades and the consuming public, demands recognition in any scheme for satisfactory settlement.   The notion that any trade may legitimately hold up other trades and block the thoroughfares of industry, because of some private quarrel between its members, is wholly indefensible.   It ignores the fact that industry is a unified organic structure, with elaborate interdependence of its parts.

Evidently, therefore, any sound arbitration must base its award upon a recognition of all the interests involved, and its process must provide for a due presentation of interests that lie outside the immediate area of conflict.   Industrial settlement cannot be secured by purely piecemeal arrangements.   Arbitration requires not only calm consideration of the particular dispute, but rules of general application to industry as a whole.   These can only be worked out by some National Industrial Council competent to survey the whole field of industry.   But there are other prerequisites to peace.   Some general Government of Industry is needed with limited powers, · (1) to secure subsistence wages and other minimum conditions for workers, (2) to own and control the operation of a few essential monopolies, (3) to secure for public revenue and communal services as large a share as is practicable of rents, excess profits and inheritances.

Such functions, in part belonging to the State, in part to

the new forms of industrial self-government, are needed to remove, or reduce, those elements of unearned or surplus wealth that everywhere are chief sources of discord, and to utilise them for strengthening the economic system and for other work of human progress.

Such is the line of argument unfolded in these chapters. I do not pretend to work out in practical detail the proposals here outlined. In such a scheme of reconstruction much must await experiment. But I have set down what appear to me to be the prime essentials of a policy of industrial peace now practicable.

I wish to express my indebtedness for some valuable suggestions and criticisms to my friend Mr. Delisle Burns, who has read this book in manuscript.

# CONTENTS

# THE CONDITIONS OF
# INDUSTRIAL PEACE

## I

## THE CAUSES OF INDUSTRIAL CONFLICTS

THE recent course of economic events has been deeply disconcerting. When the war was over, the industrial upheavals, conflicts and stoppages which ensued, were for a time accepted as the natural sequelæ of the great political and military disturbances. " It would take some time to settle down," we said, " into the pre-war grooves, and to effect the readjustments required by changes of frontiers and trade relations. Our system, with its invisible and unconscious government, would then be restored to its pre-war regularity and efficiency." This, however, has not happened, and the man in the counting-house, the street, or the House of Commons, is at a loss to explain why. His failure is partly due to overstressing the war as the cause of economic debility. The dramatic force of this mighty episode has so absorbed attention as to obscure the happenings of the preceding years. It requires an effort of memory to recall the political and industrial turbulence of the period from Mr. Lloyd George's 1909 budget to the summer of 1914. The break of nineteenth-century complacency began, however, some time before, with the rise of prices, uncompensated by the rise of money wages, from 1895 onwards. The improvement in working-class conditions since the early seventies had been fairly continuous and considerable, while the incomes of business men had been rising rapidly. But the swift advance of the United States and Germany in the heavy industries, and generally in manufacturing power, had already in the nineties menaced our supremacy in world trade, and our increasing industrial population felt the pressure of the new competition. An era of industrial unrest set in, by no means confined to this country. For the efforts of labour to grapple with the rising cost of living were manifested all over Europe in conflicts of increasing frequency and magnitude as the new century moved towards catastrophe.

But the nature of the breakdown of the competitive capitalism of the nineteenth century is misunderstood, if the labour conflict is treated as the central governing issue.

Although there is an intimate interaction between the structural changes which the industrial system was undergoing and what I may call the new industrial consciousness, it is necessary to give some separate attention to the two factors.

The free competitive market, which linked up into an effective operative system the technically independent businesses, was breaking down in most great industries before the impact of combinations. In America the Trust, in Central Europe the Cartel, in Britain a large variety of forms of combination, from the gentleman's price agreement to the full-fledged monopoly, were regulating production, controlling the price system, and interfering with that distribution of income required to maintain the regularity of industry on the old lines of *laissez-faire*. These were not, indeed, wholly novel phenomena, but the magnitude and intensity of their operations were such as to make large fissures in the economic edifice. The discovery that the new physical power of production, available in most machine-industries, showed a constant tendency to outrun demand at profitable prices, was a powerful stimulus towards the federation or union of the diminishing number of large productive units which survived the wasteful conflict of free competition. By merger, federation or agreement, the limitation of output, the fixing of prices and the division of markets, have encroached upon and superseded over considerable areas of industry the invisible government which rested upon natural harmony of separate interests. Where these combines have brought into formal union numbers of hitherto competing businesses by lateral arrangement, or have spread horizontally so as to bring in other members of a series of productive and commercial processes, large areas of conscious government have been created. Technical efficiency and elimination of waste, alike in costs of production and of marketing, are thus attainable, and under certain conditions it may pay the monopolists to fix prices lower than free competition would have left them. But, since the conscious purpose of this business government is to extract from the unified industry the maximum net profits it can be made to yield, the normal results are a restriction of production and a price considerably higher than is ' reasonable ' in the sense of being sufficient to secure an adequate supply of capital from the investment market. In other words, the industrial unity of the capitalist system is being dissolved into a number of separate autocracies whose relations with one another are essentially hostile. For every price-raising combine extorts from other industries, which need its product as raw materials, plant or power, a price that diminishes its profits, while any tax it levies on the real wages of workers in other industries by high prices of commodities either damages their standard of living or, under favouring circumstances, is thrown back upon their employers in a successful demand for higher money wages. Since industrial combination has been most successful in those departments of the metal, textile, building-materials and other industries, where larger regular demands for standard articles exists, its operations have materially affected the cost of living of the poorer classes, by depriving them of a large part of the economies of modern scientific production. An increasing proportion of the ordinary necessaries and comforts in the standard of living of the workers and middle classes, foods, clothes, housing, furniture, tobacco, amusements, is loaded with elements of surplus profits. This fact is concealed, partly by the essential secrecy with which many of the price arrangements are conducted, partly by the continued existence of numbers of small independent businesses which follow the trust prices and furnish a protective colouring. Many of the numerous processes through which raw materials pass on their journey to consumable commodities still employ the competitive price system. For though combinations in the manufacturing processes have bulked bigger in the public eye, it is in transport, distribution and finance that the new economy has scored its greatest victories. If nature has played the chief part in limiting the competition of railways, the huge capital needed for modern lines of shipping, by throwing sea-traffic more and more into a few concerns, has facilitated the price-fixing arrangements of the conference. Banking and insurance maintain a thin semblance of free competition, dividing most large and lucrative business by systems of well-recognised partitions. Wholesale and retail trade alike in most staple commodities is organised to maintain ' reasonable ' prices by regulating supplies and price agreement. Hence an increasing number of these commodities have at one or more stages of their productive and commercial journey to the consumer been held up for ransom by some organisation in control of the market whose predatory gains pass into the final selling price.

It is natural that these structural changes in industry and markets should be attended by a more active and conscious dissatisfaction with 'the capitalist system' on the part of increasing numbers of the population. Profits, regarded as the remuneration of the active organisers and risk-takers in competitive business, evoked no resentment except from socialists. But profits, got by restricting supplies and enhancing prices, produce widespread irritation among all sorts and conditions of men. One of the most distinctive outcomes of the war has been the weakening of the economic position of the professional middle-classes, who have been unable to raise the price of their services proportionately with the rise in the general level of prices, and who, in most countries, have suffered heavily by the depreciation in the value of their invested savings. This intellectual proletariat is riddled with discontent, and its more active minds are severely critical of their business masters, and the 'system' which they represent. To observant men of every class it is evident that capitalism is entering a new era of which 'organisation,' 'co-operation,' 'standardisation,' 'mass production,' are the watchwords. Germany and America have taken the lead. Even before the war the rapid advance of these countries in great industry and their growing share in the world market were causing some heart-searching in our business leaders. Chambers of Commerce were beginning to talk about scientific research, better accountancy and costing, active development of imperial and foreign markets. But it may be said that the definite acceptance of cartels and selling associations, involving organic agreements among the hitherto competing members of a trade, and the whole policy of price fixing, as methods in themselves desirable and even essential to success in modern business, has been for English business men a post-war conversion. How rapidly this new attitude of mind will mature in national organisations, and in definite membership of international cartels for the apportionment of the world's markets in raw materials and finished products, it is impossible to predict. The development of international cartels in steel and various other raw or manufactured metals such as copper, steel rails, tubes, rolled wire, in potash, dyes and other chemical products, bottles, enamel ware, incandescent mantles, sewing thread, glass and large numbers of other less important articles of commerce, opens up new possibilities of industrial peace or conflict. Primarily, such organisation makes for order and government, repressing or regulating competition of national groups in the several industries. But it is easy to see that, as in the sphere of politics, these ordered industries may develop interests and ambitions which may bring them into conflict with one another, or enable them to exercise a dangerous control over the consuming public, and over the politics of the States in which the national members of an international cartel enjoy the support of their government. At present it must suffice to recognise that a radical transformation in the capitalist structure of many of the great staple trades is taking place,[1] no longer unconsciously, but by the reasoned planning of the great industrial leaders in each country.

The earlier resentment entertained by class-conscious workers towards capitalists as sweaters and profiteers is naturally aggravated by the discovery that these same men, who pay wages below their worth, fix prices of commodities so as to reduce the value of those wages. As combination proceeds to oust competition in one large trade after another, the grip of this new capitalism will tighten, and, working

[1] Though agriculture lags behind, it is likely that the development of power-driven machinery and the growth of organisations for co-operative marketing will displace primitive competitive enterprise in the more advanced countries.

as it does with a closely welded banking system, will establish a new order of government over large areas of economic activity. It is sometimes asserted that the vast economies and high productivity achieved by such combinations, under an intelligent organisation that will take due account of the psychology of the workers, will buy off discontent with autocratic management by high wages, short hours and other good conditions of employment. 'Good conditions' will satisfy the ordinary worker, active workers (political agitators) will find successful careers within the business system, while the control of these huge enterprises will be wielded by large-minded managers and directors who will regard their enterprises as great public services rather than as profit-making businesses. This is the gospel according to Henry Ford, which has been heard gladly by many well-meaning business men here, as in America. There are some who think that America will bring this great lesson of appeasement to struggling Europe. Capitalism will socialise itself in spirit, retaining its old form, but more highly organised and with the competitive urge extracted. The rule, hitherto confined to the area of single competing businesses, will be extended to great provinces of industry, many related trades brought under a single organised finance. The good conditions of employment will perhaps include some scheme of profit-sharing or co-partnership, with an accompanying voice in the nominal control exercised by shareholders, that will secure a more effective co-operation between capital and labour in the industry. Apart from such schemes of reconciliation, the enlarged savings of the workers, evoked by higher wages, and invested through Labour Banks, or otherwise, in industry, will convert the main body of the workers into small capitalists, thus restoring the harmony of the pre-capitalist era when workers were the owners of their tools, work-place and materials. Or, with workers able to

B

accumulate capital, there seems no barrier set to the growth of a productive co-operative movement in which guilds or other groups of workmen, using their own share-capital and raising further funds by debentures or bank credits, may control and conduct businesses that are in the fullest sense ' their own.'

The pace and extent at which such schemes may fructify will mainly depend upon two speculative or imponderable factors : first, the constructive will of the workers, the intensity and persistence of their desire to reform and control the existing capitalism, and secondly, the importance of strong dominating personality in the initiation, organisation and successful conduct of business. In Britain and, indeed, throughout industrial Europe, the early possibilities of what we may term a workers' capitalism seem slight. At current wage-rates the likelihood of any large accumulation of savings by the workers is small. Profit-sharing and co-partnership have hardly passed beyond the rôle of amiable fads, and, indeed, are suspect among the main body of workers as serving to break the solidarity of trade union action and as emollients to the harshness of the profiteering system.

Thus the general result of recent movements in the structure of industry and the mentality of the workers is markedly unfavourable to industrial peace and orderly government in industry. Organised capital and labour in the several industries confront one another with a more conscious hostility than before. As in international relations, wars become less frequent but larger and more disastrous in their operations. Indeed, the substitution of trusts, cartels, combines and other associations, for competition, render the antagonism between capital and labour more reasonable. For competition, so far as it was effective, kept profits and prices low. Combination is expressly directed to raise them. This open and avowed policy of raising profits and holding up prices for the benefit of 'capitalists,' acts, as we have seen, as a natural irritant to labour. The distribution of high dividends and bonuses by highly organised combines is a factor of increasing importance in the industrial unrest. For, on the one hand, it feeds the discontent of the employees with their share of the gain, on the other, it stirs a general unrest among consumers called upon to pay high prices in order to furnish these dividends. Thus, a movement, which on its structural side marks progress in the economy of production, breeds strife among workers and consumers. The danger of the present industrial situation is thus aggravated by the more conscious antagonism between the owning and the working classes, and by a growing disillusionment alike with trade union and political action as methods of redress. The American idea, as we may call it, of an effective co-operation of capital and labour within the capitalist system, appears thus to be negatived by the mentality of labour in Britain. It is also fair to add that, except in a few enlightened quarters, there is little disposition among employers to recognise the need of any radical reforms in the relations of capital and labour, or in the conduct and control of business. The acceptance of the Trust or Combine by many of them, as conducive to an early revival of British trade, does not to their mind carry any considerable abatement of the autocratic rule of the employer, or of the right of capital to the increased gains that may result from the economies of combination. That either the workers should share in these gains by higher wages, or the public by lower prices, does not occur to the normal mind of the business man. For he is not in business for 'his health,' either of body or soul, but to make as much profit as the honest conduct of the business enables him to get. Why should he adopt an eleemosynary attitude either to his employees, who are getting 'as much as they are worth,' or to the public, who need not buy his goods if they do not care to pay his price ?

Even were it the case that the savings of British workers invested in industry gave them a substantial share in the ownership of industrial capital, this wider distribution of ownership could not be reckoned a strong security against industrial conflict. For this very multiplication of owner-ship has had important reactions upon the financial structure and control of capitalist enterprise. Increasing quantities of capital take shape in mortgages, debentures and other fixed interest securities, which carry no voice in the control of industry. A growing proportion of the savings, especially of the poorer classes, passes into industry through insurance and investment companies, leaving no direct connection between the owner and the use of capital. And, finally, the ever-growing proportion of industry and commerce, transport and finance, vested in great corporations with thousands of shareholders, by common admission leaves the latter destitute of any real part in the policy or conduct of the business, except in rare moments of emergency. Thus the actual control of business involving large capital is more and more in the hands of great financiers, managing directors and other autocrats, whose rule is endorsed by the tacit consent of the owners of the active and passive capital. The so-called conflict between capital and labour is thus a misnomer. The capitalist who really counts in the relations between ' capital and labour ' is seldom the owner of any large proportion of the capital he wields. The vast majority of capitalists are pawns in the game of a few powerful mana-gers and directors who ' run ' big business. Power figures as prominently as profits in the minds of these men, and enhanced profits are often valued primarily as the means of expanding business activities and increasing power. These considerations are of importance in enabling us to set the modern business scene and to realise the nature of the drama. For they indicate that the conflict between organised capital and organised labour is directed, not only to secure as much as possible of the gains of each business or industry for profits or for wages, but also to satisfy the lust of power. In any strongly organised Trade Union the sense of corporate power, evoked by some concrete grievance or desire for gain, generates a fighting atmosphere, which is liable to overcome all sane estimates of economic interests and possibilities in the conduct of an economic war. This psychological factor, present on both sides in organised strife, and fed by interaction, is inevitable so long as neither the opportunity nor the will exists to substitute some equitable arbitrament for the test of force. The lust for gain and for power are not, indeed, clearly separable in conduct or consciousness, for gain is an instrument of power, and power is largely realised in terms of gain. But, in considering the nature of a conflict and the possibilities of peaceful settlement, it is essential to keep in mind that the struggle for profits or better conditions of labour is always entangled and exacerbated by the self-assertive and aggressive instincts of a 'group-mind.'

Enough has been said to indicate the nature of the structural changes in modern industry and their psychological reactions which have brought about the collapse of the unseen, unconscious harmony of selfish interests that sustained the industrial system and provided a fairly effective government during the nineteenth century. Those very arts of combination, upon which we have touched, bear testimony to the waste and other defects of that invisible government, and are improvised experiments towards a more conscious and a better order. But, based as they are on considerations of narrow group interest, of employers or employed in particular businesses or industries, they are seen to afford no security of peace or prosperity to the community at large. On the contrary, their present condition, regarded from the standpoint of human security, appears analogous to the wider political groupings within the various countries, which, by repressing internal conflicts and establishing strong States, enlarged the areas of hostility and made warfare more destructive than before. In industry, as in political relations, if peace and orderly progress are to be attained, a social government which shall correlate or supplement, amend or displace, the fragmentary government of group interests must be evolved. If, as I hold, a sudden or rapid transformation into State socialism or any completely co-operative order is not practicable, the issue is that of the early adoption of what we may term 'the elements of industrial government,' in the shape of conscious plans and institutions directed primarily to secure industrial peace. In developing such plans and institution it will become evident that Peace, in industry as in political relations, is not a merely negative concept, the reconcilement of hostile forces, so as to avoid destructive action, but a positive policy of co-operation, promoting mutual gain, and evoking the mutual good will that is both cause and effect of fruitful co-operation.

But our present task is best envisaged in terms dictated by the immediate urgencies of the new situation, and addressed to getting pacific settlement of several related orders of conflict. First comes the struggle over the conditions of labour, mainly in the last resort a wage question, in the several trades. Second, the newly revealed antagonisms of interest between different classes of trades within each country, in particular between protected and exposed trades, strongly organised and weakly organised trades, agriculture and manufacture, necessary and luxury trades. Thirdly, the recent changes in the labour market show definite cleavages of interest between skilled and unskilled labour and between different sorts and grades of skill. This issue, though closely involved in the first and second conflicts, deserves separate recognition, for in any satisfactory settlement of labour conditions it provides special problems of its own. Fourthly, there stands the cluster of antagonisms that arise through the opposing interests of national groups of traders, manufacturers and investors, in foreign countries, relating to the acquisition and enjoyment of favourable access to certain essential raw materials and a 'fair share' of the export market. The tangle of these issues, generalised as 'economic imperialism,' and involving the closest union between real politics and economics in the modern world, is the gravest challenge to the art of social government.

## II

## FINDING A FAIR WAGE

THE industrial government that has passed away had, as we saw, for its governing principle free competition. That freedom, involving, as it did, intelligent mobility for all workers and owners to dispose of their labour and productive resources to the best advantage, and equal access to all markets for the disposal of commodities, was never attained in any industrial country. But in the nineteenth century considerable steps were taken towards its attainment. Everywhere free competition was qualified by monopoly, or combination or other barriers economic, political or social. But it stood as an accessible ideal. Now, instead of competition qualified by combination, we find, over an increasing area of the industrial world, combination qualified by competition.

It is this rapid transformation of the operative principle of industry that has given sharp character to the problems of conflict that confront us. Before beginning a close examination of them it is, however, essential to recognise one stiff barrier of mental attitude which obstructs, in all of them alike, policies of peaceful settlement.

The conviction, that in business every man has a 'right' to get all he can, is generally prevalent. The assertive sentiment is dormant on ordinary occasions, or is not strongly conscious in its assertion. It is supported by custom and the belief that business could not be conducted on any other principle. Hence the feeling, that we are 'right' in struggling for our 'rights,' gives a moral support to each party in a conflict of interests. For, after all, this very struggle—from the individual higgling in a market to the concerted violence of a strike or lock-out—contributes to the general harmony of the economic system. Though the contestants for ' rights ' may not clearly entertain this wider meaning of their action, it affords secret help to the maintenance of economic strife. Unless all parties to industry exert their economic force to get all they can, there is nothing to determine the conditions of production or the distribution of the product. In exceptional instances, where monopoly or favouring circumstances permit easier relations between employer and employed, some mitigation of this ' rights ' principle seems possible. But in normal business relations, as landlord, employer, worker, tradesman, consumer, each feels ' justified ' in giving as little and getting as much as he can. This is the law of the market, and, as the market is a socially useful institution, this process of bargaining seems sound.

Now the first barrier to any conscious equitable solution of our industrial troubles is the persistence of this idea, with its sentimental backing of greed, pugnacity and group feeling. Every war is hallowed by this sense of ' rights.' ' My right,' and especially ' our rights,' are ' the right,' and we should be ' wrong ' if we refused to fight for them. Ask for a definition of my right, it always comes down to ' what I can hope to get by a successful bargain.' In the last resort it is the endorsement of the famous sophism, ' Justice is the right of the stronger.' It is the maintenance of this false ethic in our economic system that blocks the path to industrial peace on every field of action. I have said that we justify our ' right ' to get all we can under the conditions of our market. But our sense of our ' rights ' carries us a good deal farther. Often actual conditions of the market seem to fail to give us our full rights. We ought to have higher wages than we can get : our capital is not earning 'reasonable' profits. In other words, it is not what we can get, but something more that is apt to figure in our consciousness when we think of our 'rights.' This 'something more' is a completely irrational element in our thinking. It is usually not the product of any calculation on our part, either of our productivity or of the funds available to pay us. It is a loose expression of a general self-appraisement of our merits, coupled with a realisation that we are unfortunately placed in the economic system. Sometimes it is the mere outcome of desire for a better living, backed by pugnacity. But wherever it crops up, and however induced, it breeds conflict.

It carries with it a misconception of the nature of the economic system. That system is a network of interrelated productive processes, each of which embodies a great heritage of traditional knowledge and skill, together with much plant and other material equipment serviceable to each process. The operation of each process involves elaborate co-operation and division of labour. Under such circumstances, it is manifestly impossible for any man, or any single group of men, to say of any serviceable product, ' I have a right to it because I made it,' or to claim that it belongs by similar right to the group of fellow-workers in a single process. Nor is it possible to measure the proportionate share which he, or they, have contributed to the making of the product. It is true that careful cost-taking may affirm that in a given process so much value has been applied to the product by the labour of a group or of a single worker. If it be held that the heritage of skill and knowledge and all the actual work of the dead past may be legitimately disregarded as 'common property' it may appear that 'his' right to the product of 'his' labour is an ascertainable quantity. But even so his real claim is not to the concrete product, the particular thing that he has made, but to its value as expressed in money payment. He claims not so many tons of coal which he has dug, or so many yards of yarn he has spun, but their value in money, what they fetch in the market. He does not, however, want that money for its own sake, but for what he can buy with it. Now, what and how much of each other commodity he can buy with the price of his labour, depends upon the skill and efficiency engaged in all the other industries making the commodities he wants to buy. This, of course, is a simple statement of the well-established truth that all value is socially determined. The productivity of each worker is socially determined, though his own will and skill are important factors in that determination : the value of the product, which is what the worker is after in his assertion of his ' rights,' is wholly determined by the social activity of the economic system as an organised whole. Now the combatant parties in an industrial conflict, between capital and labour, between strong and weak trades, between skilled and unskilled, agriculture and manufacture, national groups in the world market, one and all disregard and defy this fundamental truth of the social determination of value. Each trade, each business, employers and employed, alike claims the right, and accepts the obligation, to manage its own concerns without any outside interference, either on the part of the State or from other trades with common interests, or from the consuming public. This statement needs, of course, some qualifications. The State does intervene by various regulations, touching health and safety of workers, and in other minor matters. In recent years, more significant State action through Trade and Wages Boards, in regulating wages among a number of the less organised trades, has taken place, though in these institutions outside authority very seldom claims to override the separate self-government of the trade through its chosen representatives. The imposition of a common wage-rate by a majority of these representatives does, however, constitute a surrender of the complete autonomy of the single business. Still more significant is the establishment of the National Wage Board under the Railways Act of 1921 for the determination of wages and other conditions of employment, while the Industrial Court, set up in 1919 to determine trade disputes between employers and employed, though void of compulsory powers, marks a new considerable advance from the old position. These State interventions, however, have not as yet made any serious breach in the accepted doctrine of ' free control ' as to wages and conditions of labour, nor can they be said to have developed or expressed any new principle for that ' equitable distribution of the product,' the want of which is the main source of trouble. The general assumption still holds that every business and industry has full right of self-government, and is entitled to all the gains which it can make and equally must bear its own losses, irrespective of whether those gains or losses are attributable to its own efficiency or inefficiency, or to external causes affecting the market for its product, over which it has no control. Now this separatist view of the government of industry is in manifest contradiction to the organic unity, or close interdependence, of all industries within the economic system. The ' invisible hand ' of the older *laissez-faire* system has been withdrawn and no new organic rule has been substituted.

The success or failure of a business, its ability to pay high wages or to make high profits, is not attributable wholly, or even chiefly, to its own efficiency, as the atomistic theory pretends. It depends largely upon the number, activity and efficiency of the other businesses in the same industry. For though its productive capacity depends upon its own equipment, technique, organisation and the efficiency of its personnel, the amount of its output and sales depends largely upon what the other competing businesses are capable of doing, and the total amount of business there is to do. And these are not matters within its own control. But not only does its material output depend upon the condition of the whole industry; the price it obtains for its product, and, therefore, the rates of wages and of profits it can pay, depend upon the demand for the commodity. And, finally, the value of the money wages and profits that are obtainable, i.e. the real wages and profits, depends upon the efficiency and productivity of all the other businesses and industries which make up the economic system. Under such conditions, what is the use of pretending that each business must be held wholly responsible for paying its own way and wholly justified in taking all it can get by selling its product ? Let me illustrate by the case of the coal stoppage. Here was a quarrel about wages and hours (primarily wages) between employers and workers in a fundamental industry. Though other workers butted in for a short spell, and the Government made a few hesitant overtures for peace, the initial attitude of the business classes and the general public was that mine-owners and miners must settle among themselves or fight it out, and that other trades and the domestic consumer must put up with any incidental losses and inconveniences, since they had no *locus standi* in the issue. This initial attitude has changed. As the effects of the coal stoppage spread, causing paralysis in the iron and steel trades and other great coal users, cutting down the supply and raising the price of power, heat, lighting and transport, forcing every home to rigorous economy of fuel, alarm and indignation arose at the danger and absurdity of this public impotence. Was it possible to acquiesce in a situation where the private quarrel between employers and workers in an essential industry could bring ruin to other industries, threaten social order and imperil public finance, without any right of intervention on the part of any of these vital interests ? Never has there been a more striking testimony to the need of some conscious regulation of the industrial system in virtue of its social or organic unity. The new attitude demands that it shall be made impossible for any industry or other service, upon the regular functioning of which other great industries and even the subsistence of a whole people depend, to cease its operation because its members quarrel about terms of employment. This right of private war must disappear from industry : rival groups must no longer be permitted to block the thoroughfares of industry and endanger the safety of peaceful citizens. Why should an association of employers or a union of employees, or both, in a particular industry, quarrelling over rates of remuneration, be allowed to stop mills in other industries and throw out of employment men who have no part in the quarrel and are not consulted on a matter that is of vital moment to them ?

The absolute right to lock-out or to strike must go. It is unjust, in that it is an appeal to force in a matter of disputed right : it is inhuman, because of the misery it causes to the workers : it is wasteful of the resources of capital and labour : it is wicked, because it stirs up hate : it is anti-social in that it denies and disrupts the solidarity of the community. Common sense, as well as the finer feelings for peace, humanity and equity, demands that industrial disputes, which cannot find amicable settlement between the parties immediately concerned, must be submitted to some impartial board or court, whose award must, if the pressure of public opinion does not suffice for settlement, be made compulsory. This is the demand for what may be here conveniently termed compulsory arbitration, leaving open for the present the question of wage-boards *versus* tribunals. It is based upon the principle that the settlement of a trade dispute, being a social interest, demands a method of settlement compatible with that principle.

Now the stubborn refusal hitherto of most business men and most workers to admit the right, utility or necessity, of any such ' outside ' interference, is not wholly due to their failure to recognise the organic nature of industry, as involving other industries and the consuming public in the consequences of a stoppage in ' their ' trade. Other ideas and feelings are involved, which deserve consideration. The sense of ownership, of possessing the right ' to do with our own as we please ' (apart from factory regulations, etc.), is supported by all the prestige and moral authority which law gives to property. To tell a mill-owner that he is not to have the right to close his mill, without the consent of some public authority, is not only an encroachment upon his time-honoured legal rights but a shock to his sense of the sacredness of property. If he thinks he can force upon his employees a reduction of wages, or an increase of hours, by means of a lock-out, he is convinced he ought to have the ' right ' to take this course, irrespective of any damage it may do to other trades from which he buys or to which he sells. So he is fundamentally indisposed to submit to any outside authority the question whether he can under existing conditions, or by better management, pay the wages his employees demand. The reasons he will assign will be plausible : he will plead that no outside authority can have the intimate knowledge of his business and his market that is essential to a sound award, that an award imposed upon him will weaken his authority and the discipline necessary for the efficient conduct of his works, and that no settlement, except one voluntarily reached by the parties concerned, will give any security against future trouble. There is something substantial in these objections. They come to this, that a settlement by consent between the two parties before the issue has become inflamed and obdurate, is far preferable to a settlement by trial of strength. But the demand for compulsory arbitration does not deny the preferability of such conciliation : it merely insists that where conciliation is not effected, the issue should not be fought out by a strike or lock-out, but settled by the provided tribunal. The employer's reluctance to admit this *dernier ressort* is mainly due to an offended sense of personal property and power. The factory is his and he has a right to settle the terms on which it shall be worked.

This interpretation is borne out by the similar attitude of labour, complicated, however, by one or two other considerations. The worker's sense of property in his labour power has more natural force behind it than the owner's sense of property, which, except when it is the direct product of his own personal effort, has more the character of a legal than a natural right. Labour is the direct expression of a personality and carries the strongest feeling of possession. A man who sells his labour is selling himself : his right to refuse to sell, unless the terms of sale are satisfactory to him, has the appearance of an absolute right. It is valued the higher because, for the vast majority of workers, it is their only property. To tell a worker, then, that he must not decide for himself the terms on which he shall work, but must leave them to be determined by some outside authority, whose award he shall be bound to accept, appears to him unjust and intolerable. His right to strike is to him a matter of personal liberty. And, if he has the right to say upon what terms he will work, and to refuse to work if he cannot get them, so he claims the right to take joint action with his fellow-workers in the assertion of these rights. So the members of a trade union in an essential industry claim the right to take an action for the furtherance of their own 'legitimate' interests which damages the entire economic system and the life of the community, without these wider interests having any 'right' of intervention. Either an employers' association, or a trade union, insists, then, upon its 'right' to refuse the use of its capital or its labour, and to disregard the reactions of the stoppage upon the economic system as a whole.

But the full difficulty of the situation is only seen when the central issue of wage-fixing is approached. A wage is a particular form of price. Now right through the economic system, as normally operated, prices are fixed by the interplay of demand and supply in each market, the suppliers exercising the right to withhold their goods if the price offered by the demanders fails to yield them a reasonable profit. Even where combinations of merchants limit supplies and raise prices, so as to yield excessive profits, public control is rarely exercised, so strong is the convention that supply and demand should be allowed full scope in price-fixing. Though the special emergencies of war, and great public disturbances, have forced the intervention of the State in the rationing of goods and the limitation of prices, the general sentiment in every country is unfavourable to such intervention, partly because it is 'outside interference with private business,' partly because it is believed to be inefficient and economically dangerous. "Why then," say the workers, "should you select a particular class of markets, labour markets, in order to claim a public right to supervise or fix prices ? Although you are aware that the prices of meat, flour, fish, tobacco, milk and a great variety of other commodities are fixed under conditions of combination or unfree competition, you do not insist that the State or other outside authority should regulate these prices. You respect the vested interests of property in all these trades, and carry your interference with them no farther than occasional inquiry and publicity,

c

why then should you seek in labour markets alone, where you are dealing with the poorer classes of the community, to dictate a price settlement ? " This attitude of mind among workers is supported by other considerations of class suspicion, always natural and sometimes justified. They suspect of class-bias the mentality of the official, or the lawyer, appointed to arbitrate, by reason of his social position, and his lack of sympathetic understanding of important aspects of working-class life : his language and bearing are those of the master-class, his very efforts after sympathy and understanding of their case breed suspicion. They fear they will be outwitted in the presentation and argument of their case. And this is likely, for their common refusal to employ expert and highly feed counsel leaves them at the mercy of trade union officials, selected for quite other qualities than the capacity of close formal argument, often involving legal technicalities. These men, save in rare instances, are quite unfitted to cross-examine the Company's accountant, in such wise as to make the labour case effective. For, in enforcing the demand for higher wages, or in resisting a cut, the relevant facts are precisely those with which labour is from its very position most unfamiliar. It is a dim consciousness of this unfamiliarity that makes them suspicious of the whole procedure. It is true that wages and conciliation boards are widely used instruments, and, where there is reasonable publicity of accounts and market conditions, good settlements result. But the case we are considering is that where conciliation fails, and we ask whether under such circumstances the trade union mentality favours compulsory arbitration. If we put the issue in the simpler form, ' Are the workers willing to abandon the right to strike ? ' the normal present answer is a plain negative. They still insist on the final right to decide the price at which they will sell their labour-power. Their present insistence is ultimately based upon (1) a natural disposition to believe that they are underpaid, and that apparently prosperous employers could afford to pay them more, and (2) the recognition that the only way of asserting their right successfully is by the exercise of superior economic pressure, in default of any equitable and pacific mode of settlement in sight.

This, however, it may be said, begs the question. Suppose it were proposed to set up fairly constituted Trade Boards or Arbitration Tribunals, and to give them statutory powers to settle wage-disputes, would the two parties be ready to accept and to abandon their right of private war ? Experience in Australia, New Zealand [1] and America leaves the answer doubtful. The willingness of labour seems based less on acceptance of an equitable principle than upon a calculation as to the probability of an immediate wage-rise, and that in its turn depends upon the measure of industrial prosperity and of prices. Where industry is improving, the workers consider that by resort to the Court they can get a larger or earlier advance than by the more hazardous method of the strike. Where industry declines, the employers seek a corresponding gain in the enforcement of earlier or larger reductions than negotiations or even a lock-out would be likely to yield.

"Employers probably accept compulsory arbitration," writes Mrs. E. M. Burns, "only because it is the lesser of two evils. The attitude of workers in Australia is similarly determined by the chance of obtaining greater benefit under any other system. Thus the unorganised and sweated workers are unanimously in favour of the retention of wage regulation ; the more organised workers, who in Australia assume great importance, regard it merely as a palliative

[1] Cf. Mr. Pember Reeves's *State Experiments in Australia and New Zealand* (George Allen and Unwin).

which should be made use of only so long as labour is not strong enough to introduce more drastic changes." [1]

Compulsory arbitration, again, is no complete method of settlement, unless it carries with it compulsory acceptance of the award. It is not, however, possible to enforce wage payments upon employers which they genuinely hold themselves unable to pay, or to force them to keep a factory going at a loss. It is not possible to prevent them from closing down unprofitable works. Nor is it easier to compel a man to work at wages he does not deem adequate, or even to prevent an organised strike against the acceptance of an unpopular award. This has been the experience of Australia, and it would be ours unless a much stronger public opinion, both among employers and employed, support these methods of industrial peace. A fine, as a penalty, difficult of enforcement from an employer, whose contention was that the wage-award made his business unprofitable, would be impossible in the case of individual workers. The demand that the union fund should be attached for payment of the fine would not prove an effective enforcement of a wage-award which individual workers were not willing to accept. No union could coerce its members into working, and a fine levied on the general fund of the union would dissolve the union, and leave no future basis of collective bargaining, conciliation and arbitration.

The initial obstacle, not yet surmounted by any State experiments, is the failure to secure a generally accepted principle for the determination of a ' living,' a ' fair,' or a ' reasonable ' wage. If it were possible to get agreement upon a minimum, living or subsistence wage, it might seem possible to build upon this foundation a series of differential wages representing ' fair ' remuneration for various sorts and degrees of skill, disagreeability and other factors in class

[1] *Wages and the State,* p. 408 (P. S. King & Son).

and individual wages. But the physiological analysis upon which it has been sought to base a 'living' or a 'subsistence' wage, is vitiated by several considerations. In the first place, physiologists and dieticians are widely divided on the kinds, quantities and composition of foods for various sorts of workers and their families. The important though mysterious element of vitamins has qualified to an unknown extent the old reliance upon calories, and the accepted proportions between proteids, fats and carbo-hydrates. Moreover, a 'living' wage must always share the indefiniteness that attaches to life itself. The length, strength and fulness of life must all enter into the conception of a living wage. In every attempt to discriminate between necessaries, conveniences, comforts, luxuries, much overlapping appears. Some, not only conveniences, but comforts and luxuries, are strictly conducive to the vigour and worth of life. The attempts of Mr. Rowntree and others to make allowances for non-physiological 'human needs' in a living wage do not go far towards a solution of our difficulty. Mrs. Burns gives an instructive account of the fumblings of Australian judges in interpretation of the Living Wage as prescribed in their Acts. "Thus in 1905 Mr. Justice Heydon defined the Living Wage as enough to enable the worker to live *a human life*, to marry and bring up a family, and maintain them and himself with, at any rate, *some small degree of comfort*; and later in the same year he spoke of a 'fair living wage' as an idea which conveyed a definite meaning. Even after many attempts had been made to translate the standard into concrete terms, the various Acts preferred to adopt vague phrases which could be more easily adjusted to the prevailing ideas of what constituted 'fair,' 'reasonable' or 'comfort.' Thus the West Australian Act of 1922 prescribed a Living Wage which should allow the recipient to live in 'reasonable comfort,' while we find a

variant of the same idea in the 1912 Industrial Arbitration
Act of South Australia, when the Living Wage is defined as
a sum 'sufficient for *the normal and reasonable needs* of an
average employee living in the locality where the work under
consideration is done. . . . In 1916 the Queensland Act
referred to a '*fair and average standard of comfort* having
regard to the conditions of living among employees in the
calling.' In 1920 the New Zealand Arbitration Act
prescribed 'a *fair* living wage,' and in the following year the
Amending Act spoke of a *fair* standard of living." [1]

All these definitions assume that something more than
physical subsistence is involved. Not bare life but some
standard of life is assumed. This is certainly the accepted
view in Britain. " A living wage, as ordinarily conceived,
is a wage that will enable the working man who receives it,
if he has an average family to maintain and if he has average
good fortune in the matter of sickness, to earn an income
sufficient for a good life." [2] What is goodness in a life?
A 'good' life for a worker earning a normal wage of £2 a
week will differ from that of a worker with £4 a week,
and so on through all the higher levels of income. 'Goodness' is even more indefinite than such terms as 'decency'
or 'comfort.'

It is easy, however, to scoff at the vague variety of this
phrasing, but if we are to start with any conception of a
'living' or a 'subsistence' or a 'fair' wage, we must posit
a conception of 'a life worth living,' the term implying
something above the physical subsistence level. How much?
Reasonable reference might be made to the prevailing notion
about 'worth' in the grade of society to which the worker
belongs. But that reference could not be final. Healthy
housing conditions, as interpreted by any sanitary authority,

[1] *Wages and the State*, p. 301.
[2] Pigou, *Economics of Welfare*, ed. 1, p. 541.

will condemn the house accommodation accepted as sufficient by large numbers of workers. So with other hygienic requirements, for example, the adequate use of milk in children's diet. If, therefore, civilised society is to deal with wage settlement, with a minimum living wage for its starting point, it is likely to be drawn on to a wage-level which will approach, if it does not exceed, 'what the trade will bear.' Indeed, the chief objection raised by our statistical economists to the demands of the workers for a higher standard of comfort is that the total income of industry is not large enough to bear the increased wage-bill.

If we turn from a Living Wage, equivalent to, or based upon, bare physical subsistence, to the concept of a 'Fair Wage,' which generally aims at a higher level than bare subsistence, we find ourselves in even graver difficulties. Dr. Marshall's definition of fairness, to the effect that wages in any occupation are fair when " they are about on a level with the payment made for tasks in other trades which are of equal difficulty and disagreeableness, which require equally rare natural abilities and an equally expensive training," [1] does not carry us far. First, there arises the difficulty of finding any acceptable measure of the skills, natural abilities, difficulty and agreeability, of different sorts of work, other than the compensative rates of remuneration which are the actual matter in question. But, if this difficulty be surmounted, and it be agreed that several sorts of work, A, B, C are 'about on a level,' as regards the remuneration they should receive, though they differ widely in their actual wage-rates, what help does Dr. Marshall's definition render ? Is the 'fair' wage the average of A, B and C, or the highest of the three wages, or what ?

If the assumption is that the mobility of labour is such that labour tends to equalise the net advantages in different

[1] Introduction to L. L. Price's *Industrial Peace.*

occupations, so that most kinds of work are in this sense equally remunerated, forming a ' norm,' to which some exceptional and ' unfairly ' paid trades should be brought into conformity, one can only say that there is no reason to hold that any such mobility and equality of net advantages exists. It would be ridiculous to suggest that the wage-rate of a bricklayer, as compared with that of a southern agricultural labourer, is explained by any of these differential considerations. Manifestly it is due to organisation, planned scarcity, and consequent bargaining power. To say that A's wage is ' unfairly ' low, because B's and C's are considerably higher, may be quite unwarranted. For it may be contended that B's and C's wages are ' unfairly ' high. Again, suppose that A's wage-rate is upon the same level with that of B, C and other workers of presumably equal conditions of skill, agreeability, etc., is that to be taken as conclusive evidence that A's wages are ' fair ' ? The main case for workers is based upon the contention that, normally and generally, employers (if equally well organised) have advantages in bargaining with labour. At any rate this may hold of any group of trades, including A, B and C. In such event fairness is not assured by saying that A is as well off as B and C. Though a ' fair ' wage is apt to present itself to any grade of workers as a wage as high as that paid to *any* other grade whose work is not visibly harder, more skilful, dangerous, irregular, than their own, such a view could hardly be taken by an arbitrator as the basis of an award under the existing wage system. For the valid objection might be raised that the higher wage-rate was ' more than the trade could bear.'

The rejoinder that the higher wage-bill, by reacting on the higher efficiency of the workers, and on the inventiveness, better organisation and other economies of management, will make the business able to bear the rise of wages, is not always convincing. The strength and quickness of these reactions will differ widely in different businesses. The Fordist philosophy is not applicable to all cases, to none perhaps with the same force and pace as to the American automobile industry. Those who are out for a ' fair wage ' in all trades must be prepared to find some trades which can not meet the demand out of their own resources, at any rate when trade is bad. What is an Arbitration Court to do when it is confronted with such a case ? Is it to declare against the claims for a fair wage, or even a ' living ' wage, on the ground that the trade or some businesses cannot pay ? Or is it to adopt the principle that a trade or a business must pay a living wage or cease to exist ? The first decision is an offence against humanity and the accepted view that ' sweating ' is a social wrong, injurious not merely to its immediate victims but to the body politic. The second decision may lead to the extinction of a useful business or trade temporarily suffering from causes outside its own control, or otherwise requiring time to make adjustments that would enable it to pay the living wage. Extinction would also signify an additional burden thrown upon the nation for the temporary or permanent maintenance of the unemployed workers. Where it is not a question of temporary depression but of lasting weakness, the common-sense verdict, that a trade or business which cannot pay its way must make place for one that can, may perhaps be accepted. It may be wise for us to hold that we will not have sweated industries in our national system, even if it means that the products of sweated industries will be imported from other countries.

The net effect of this investigation, so far as it has gone, is to show that a trade dispute in which the issue is a ' minimum,' a ' living,' a ' fair ' wage, or simply a wage-increase or reduction, is incapable of reasonable or equitable settlement by confining the consideration of the case to the trade directly involved. A wage-increase, awarded on grounds of 'sweating,' or to bring wages to the level paid in other similar occupations, may, if it does not provide its own fund out of increased efficiency of labour or of organisation, be passed on to the consumer in a rise of prices, causing also some unemployment in the trade owing to reduced purchases at the higher price. The higher price, due to the wage-increase, will mean some reduction in the real income of all other workers, i.e. the purchasing power of their wages has fallen. Coal is a case in point. If higher wages of miners meant higher price of coal, other workers are called upon to pay part, or most, of the higher wage of miners, in the higher price of coal. If this is not immediately made good in a general rise of money-wages, it means reduced purchases of food, clothing and other articles consumed by the public, and some shrinkage of production and unemployment in all trades affected thus. The effect of higher coal-prices will also operate on all other branches of industry, especially transport, manufacture and power services, raising their costs of production and (except in the case of businesses screened from competition and earning high profits) the prices for their goods or services. Thus a double flow of economic causation will tend to lower the real income of the rest of the community, in order to raise miners' wages.

This line of reasoning seems to warrant the conclusion that by a wage-rise the miners could only gain at the expense of other workers. But before accepting it, two other lines of reasoning should be explored. In the first place, as we have already indicated, it is not inevitable that coal-prices should rise proportionately with the rise of wages, if at all. Improved efficiency and organisation, stimulated by the higher wages, might produce a compensating economy, though this would take time. So far as this occurred, no considerable rise of coal-prices need occur, and all the effects we have named would be proportionately reduced or cancelled. This argument assumes that, owing to other economies in this particular industry, an increased product might be created out of which the higher wage-bill could be met. But the increased production need not be confined to coal. Absolutely the first effect of higher wages would be, not the raising of the price of coal (if it were raised), but the putting of increased consuming-power into the hands of miners. The exercise of this increased demand for goods issuing from miners would stimulate activity in the industries producing these goods, increase the volume of employment, raise prices and evoke increased efficiency of production. In other words, the total pool of wealth, from which the miners appear to be drawing an increased amount, is not a fixed pool, but is itself increased by the sequence of events set in action by the rise of miners' wages. When we consider that the stimulus to increased production spreads from one trade to another, through linkage both of consumers' and producers' demands, we realise that the arbitrator who might be called upon to assess a ' fair ' or ' reasonable ' wage in any trade could not properly perform his task unless he took into consideration the indirect effects of his award. Other trades have a right to be heard in any case which may effect their ' vital ' interests by reducing their share of the general pool of wealth out of which the wages of each group is paid.

But the intimate interdependence of trades bears upon the wage dispute within a single trade in quite another way. The reason why employers are unable to pay a ' fair ' wage may be that some of their other ' costs,' such as raw materials, or power, are raised by the price-control exercised by other industries vested with monopoly or other high bargaining power. In point of fact, every monopoly or quasi-monopoly, exercised by a trust or combine, or the holders of some scarce opportunity, which enables them to extort a high price, is making it difficult and sometimes impossible for competitive businesses to pay a fair wage. For the aggregate effect of these trust and combine prices is to increase their pull upon the aggregate real income of the community and proportionately to reduce the pull of the uncombined and weaker trades. This being so, it follows that, in what appears at first sight a narrowly confined conflict between employers and employed in a single business or industry, the wider issue of a struggle between strong and weak trades is involved. This is not, indeed, always the case. In times of general prosperity a wage-dispute may often turn on a demand of labour for a share in the high profits which a rise of prices has placed in the employers' hands. This is sometimes only a demand that money-wages shall be raised so as to keep pace with the rising level of prices. But it may be a demand for a share in a 'surplus' due to the full activity and special prosperity of the business or trade. In that case it would seem that the wage demand may be met by a simple consideration of its magnitude in relation to the available surplus. Here it would seem needless to go outside the trade in making an award. But the real difficulty in arbitrating such a demand is great. For there exists no principle for the distribution of such a surplus as between capital and labour. Whereas a wage of efficiency and a rate of interest adequate to maintain capital or to evoke an increase may be calculable quantities, a 'surplus' is strictly an irrational quantity which meets no needs and is normally distributed by economic force. It generally comes first in the form of high profits, and then labour gets a share when it can bring organised force to bear, with the menace of a strike always in the background. But when we are considering arbitration as a method of equitable apportionment of that surplus, we can find no principle for its allocation. No equitable division seems possible, because the thing itself is not endowed with equity in its origin. These surpluses are either the results of contrived or of adventitious rises of price. Where close combination exists, they may result from restriction of output, joined with economies of business organisation, issuing in prices that yield a wide margin of profit. Even when, as is often the case, it is claimed that, since technical improvements and skilful management or finance have helped to make the ' surplus,' it belongs by right to capital and enterprise, there exists no measurable relation between the surplus and the necessary payments for these displays of skill and enterprise. Some of the ' surplus ' may reasonably be allocated to these payments, but how much ? The modern State has already begun to contemplate these irrational funds with a covetous eye. But it ought to be clear that here exists a body of income which, social in origin, in its effect on prices is especially fitted for meeting the defects of an unregulated wage system, by redressing the balance between strong and weak trades and well-organised and ill-organised labour.

In an economic system where the principle prevails that every business must always pay its way out of its own resources and is entitled to retain for its profits all that low wages or favourable markets enable it to get, there can be no settlement of our industrial conflicts. We have adduced the proposals and experiments in *ad hoc* arbitration in order to enforce the truth that no satisfactory settlement is possible by a Board or Court confining its inquiry to the conditions of the particular case. Amid the intricacies of an elaborately interrelated industrial system each industry, each trade, each wage-earner, is pulling to get the largest share he can out of the aggregate pool, and what he can and does get depends on the size of the pool and the strength of his pull. But there is little to correlate this pulling power to skill, or effort, or needs, nothing to secure that what he gets is a 'fair' wage or a 'fair' profit. It is easy to see that some are injuriously underpaid, others wastefully overpaid, but these particular excesses and defects cannot be estimated, still less remedied, without taking account of the general pool on which they draw and to which their particular productive activities contribute.

Let me summarise the argument so far as it has gone.

There is a wide and growing dissatisfaction with the settlement of disputes on wages and other conditions of labour between employers and employed by methods of force, involving strikes or lock-outs. If negotiation between the two parties fails to secure agreement, the issue should be put to an impartial court or tribunal. But any real attempt to ascertain the principles on which such an impartial body should decide the issue is baffled, on the one hand, by the vagueness and uncertainty attaching to such terms as 'living' or 'minimum' or 'fair' wage, on the other, by the absence of any basis of distribution where a business is earning a 'surplus' rate of profit, and labour demands a share. These difficulties are seen to be inherent in the notion that a business is an independent being, separate for all financial purposes from any other business, the truth being that the actual finance of any business, the amount of its spendings on what it has to buy and of its takings from what it has to sell, are intimately related to the productive operations and the finance of other businesses, not only in its own industry, but in all other industries which go to compose the economic system. In any wage-dispute an arbitral award, which raised or lowered wages in a trade or business, is seen to affect for gain or loss the wages and profits in other trades and businesses, through raising or lowering the prices of articles which enter into the costs of production in these other industries and so influencing wages throughout the economic system. Thus it appears that no just and reasonable settlement is possible by an arbitral or other body which confines its inquiry to the conditions of the particular business or trade where the dispute has arisen. The intricate unity of the industrial system requires that the direct and indirect reactions of an award applicable to a single business or trade upon other businesses or trades shall be taken into account. Such an inquiry soon discloses the conflicting interests between strongly organised and weakly organised trades, trades concerned exclusively in supplying the home market and trades engaged in foreign markets. It thus appears that, since every wage-dispute in a single business or trade signifies a demand for a larger share of the general body of wealth, it cannot be settled equitably apart from other claims upon this same body of wealth. In a word, the just settlement of a wage-dispute requires the acceptance and application of a just principle for the distribution of the general income.

# III

## THE POOL OF WEALTH

IF the settlement of wage-disputes, envisaged as industrial peace and justice, depends upon the right distribution of the general income, the pool of wealth, it may well appear that we have only substituted a larger for a smaller problem and found no solution. Up to a certain point, however, the principle of distribution according to needs is admitted. In most orderly communities it is applied, so far as to secure the bare physical subsistence of all members. In England, for example, Poor Law relief, the unemployment 'dole,' old age pensions, Employers' Liability Acts, provision of free meals under the Education Acts, must be regarded as contributions to the acceptance of this principle. The experiments in Family Allowances in various countries, and the strong support given to this policy in Britain to-day, avowedly find their justification in a principle of distribution according to needs. When we come to the conceptions of 'minimum,' 'basic,' 'fair' or 'reasonable' wages, the principle of needs is crossed and qualified by the principle of distribution according to productivity, that term taking into account strength, ability, skill, expense of training, and other qualities said to affect the 'value' of the particular sort of work. To some extent, indeed, these differential wages of classes and individuals may also be resolved into payments based on need. Where skill and training require a considerable outlay of time and money, some extra payment for such work may be considered as interest on personal capital needed to evoke the skill. There is, however, no ground for supposing that actual differential wages (class or individual) are accurate measures of this element of need. Most of them have an element of scarcity value, due to restricted opportunity of access into skilled employments, or to natural endowments of brain or muscle. The reduction of the difference between skilled and unskilled wages in most countries during recent years testifies to a considerable 'artificial' element in the class wages that hitherto prevailed, and there is good reason to suppose that, with more mobility and equality of access to educational opportunities, the differences of class wages will continue to shrink. But this movement is likely to be slow and partial, in view of the strong bargaining power of labour in sheltered trades and in public employment, and the development of trusts and cartels may be accompanied by a high wage policy, making for inequality of distribution among workers as a body.

Minimum-wage Boards, Trade Boards, 'fair' wages clauses in public contracts, and wages for public employees, are all expressly, though not exclusively, directed to adjust payments according to needs. In some cases a narrow significance is given to 'needs,' which keeps the wage-award close to bare physical subsistence, but there is a growing tendency to a more liberal view which seeks to stretch needs to cover some of the conveniences and comforts of a 'civilised life.' A striking example of the elasticity of the 'needs' basis is found in the deliberate recognition of a social status and expenditure proper to the higher officials in municipal and State services, to be taken into account in the salary attaching to such posts. From these various sources converging lines of testimony indicate the growing strength of the idea and feeling that workers are performing a social function, and that their pay must have regard to the maintenance of their fitness for the performance of that function. This idea and feeling may at first sight seem far-fetched and

D

foreign to the normal labour contract. But the growth of a conscious labour movement has combined with a clearer perception of the moral defects of the bargaining process between rich and poor, strong and weak, to press towards a revision of the distribution of the general income in the direction of distribution according to needs. But it is already clear from what has been said that ' needs ' is not a fixed but an elastic term. To provide a sufficient quantity and variety of pure and wholesome food for the requirements of a family, with decent clothing for all weathers, and housing that is sufficient in space, number of rooms and hygienic conditions, is in itself a demand considerably in excess of the provision possible for half our working population under the existing wage system. If we added what are regarded by middle-class people as ' necessities of life,' good medical assistance available at home, fairly frequent holidays and ' reasonable recreations,' books and newspapers, etc., taking into account fulness of life as well as mere physical duration, we should reach a level of ' needs ' far beyond the limits of the existing ' pool of wealth,' however equitably distributed. This obliges us to look a little closer at the claims for a distribution according to needs. ' Needs ' may have a narrower or a broader connotation, according as productive efficiency, or ' a good life,' is the gauge. The two meanings no doubt interpenetrate and overlap. But in approaching distribution from the standpoint of wages, it is best to consider first the narrower meaning.

The claim of any body of workers upon ' the pool,' in virtue of their needs, will thus signify the real wages that are physically and morally necessary to evoke and maintain the largest quantity and best quality of output of their productive energy. I use the term ' morally necessary ' because a wage of mere physiological sufficiency may not be an adequate incentive. And it is this adequate incentive to which we must look for our interpretation of economic needs. If a man were a mere machine that would work by converting so much fuel into industrial energy, the necessary wage would be a closely calculable cost. But, as a converter of food into labour-power, every man differs in some degree from every other, and the requirements of his family still more. Moreover, every man requires some margin (and a differing one) of human satisfaction over and above the physiological limit, in order to evoke his 'will to work.' Thus elements of personal difference and of human needs are found to enter into what may be called 'a wage of efficiency,' that wage which an intelligent employer will in his own interest pay.

But, when we are considering the whole problem of distribution of the pool, we shall keep separate, as far as we can, the claim of economic needs, the wage of efficiency, from the wider claim on grounds of human well-being. For this wider claim, so far as it is a pull upon the fund of wealth, may be, and in some considerable measure is, met by communal expenditure and not out of wages. But if we regard this economic wage, based on physical and moral needs, as a first claim upon the 'pool,' we must bear in mind that neither ' needs ' nor ' pool ' is a fixed quantity, and that in fact they are interdependent factors. Needs, both physiological and moral, grow with more knowledge of hygiene and life, enhancing the productive efficiency of workers. The 'pool' grows larger, in part from the improved efficiency and co-operation of producers, and enables ' needs ' to be satisfied more fully. So far as population is under some control, a natural harmony thus seems to be established between the pool of wealth and a wage-payment based on needs. There is thus a *prima facie* case for adjudication in a wage-dispute, so far as the demand for higher wages, or the resistance of a wage-cut, is based on

' economic needs,' seeking expression in a wage of subsistence or of efficiency. If this claim in any business or trade cannot be met out of the resources of that business or trade, owing to causes that lie outside its own control, there is a reasonable claim upon the larger general ' pool,' provided that the business or trade is one that should be kept alive in the public interest.

The strong animus against the idea of a public subsidy to wages is attributable to several causes. First, there is a reasonable fear lest such a subsidy may serve to bolster up inefficiency of organisation, technique or management, in a business or industry, or may support a policy of slackness or ca' canny on the part of labour. For though the subsidy may be claimed upon the ground that the unremunerative state of the trade is due to external causes, internal inefficiency may be a contributory factor, and one effect of a subsidy will be to remove or diminish the incentive to internal reform. The coal trade is here again a case in point. While public impolicy may be regarded as a chief cause of its evil plight, internal slackness was a contributory cause, and the public subsidy of 1925–6 acted as a drug instead of a stimulus to reconstruction. It will not be easy to apportion the responsibility for trade misfortunes between external and internal causes. Secondly, it will be urged that, where a fall of prices, rendering the whole or a large section of a trade unable to pay ' fair ' wages, is due either to an excess of productive power or to a shrinkage of the market, a subsidy will serve to keep in operation plant and labour which ought to be closed down. In other words, a policy of subsidies might injuriously stereotype the size and character of trades, interfering with the flow of capital and labour into more socially serviceable channels.

Both these objections rest upon the assumption that a subsidy cannot be, or in effect would not be, confined to its proper task of compensation for injuries arising from political or economic causes outside the trade to which the subsidy is paid. But is it impossible to conceive an expert body of impartial arbitrators, capable of distinguishing cases of external injury from cases of internal inefficiency, and of utilising a subsidy for the purpose of stimulating efficiency, and, if necessary, of assisting to reduce the size of an overgrown trade, and helping its excessive members to transfer themselves to other occupations? Remember there are only bad alternatives, if wisely applied subsidies are impracticable. One is that 'sweating' or 'unfair' wages should continue to be paid. Another is that strikes or lock-outs should continue to occur, incapable of satisfactory settlement between the parties. A third is that the trade or a large section of it, unable to pay out of its own resources the wage awarded by a board or tribunal, will go out of business, leaving a body of unemployed to be supported during a period of idleness upon dole or poor relief, themselves worse forms of public subsidy. The alternative of the subsidy rests on the contention that there are trades which it is socially desirable to keep alive at their present size, or with some reduction, but that, owing to passing conditions of their market, they are temporarily unable to pay minimum subsistence wages and meet their other necessary obligations.

Those who insist upon the invalidity of every subsidy may, perhaps, argue that well-regulated businesses should be able and willing to make provision out of 'good times' for 'bad times,' setting aside reserves from profitable years to maintain wages as well as dividends in unprofitable years. They will not, it can be urged, be encouraged to take this sound far-sighted policy, if their temporary misfortunes can be made the basis of a claim for an outside subsidy. And this is true. An application for a subsidy should not be entertained, unless ordinary business foresight has been exercised by its managers, so as to enable them to meet ordinary trade fluctuations without letting down the wages below a 'fair' level. Subsidies are not a method of dealing with the ordinary 'ups' and 'downs' of trade, but for injuries against which no adequate provision was possible.

Subsidies have two proper functions. They may be applied to help an industry to pay its way in cases of unforeseen temporary emergency, and to help in letting down an overgrown industry where its overgrowth was attributable to public policy (as in over-stimulated war-trades), or to unpredictable declines of the market. In a word, if the avoidance of industrial conflicts is to be averted by some equitable provision for subsistence-wages in a trade, cases will arise where outside pecuniary assistance will be necessary. It is justified, firstly, by the broad principle that the funds received within the trade to support its 'costs' are always to a large extent determined by influences from the demand side, i.e. by the general conditions of other industries and the incomes they yield. It is justified, secondly, by the consideration that the injuries, or emergencies, which render a trade unable to pay its way are often due to wars, monetary policies, tariffs or other public acts, or to quite unpredictable economic events in the outside world. In an economic system so constituted, the admitted principle that the subsistence of workers, and, so far as possible their continuous employment, should be secured, involves some call upon the general fund of wealth to supplement wages in such trade emergencies.

But it is evident that the limits to this adoption of distribution according to needs must be carefully explored. Belonging, as it does, to the 'functional' conception of work, we have to consider how far 'human nature' in its economic aspect responds to this conception. How far is it possible to pay workers without express regard to the amount and

quality of work they do ? Most work is, and will continue
to be, dull, tiring and otherwise undesirable in itself, though
these disagreeabilities may be mitigated by shorter hours,
change of work or other improved conditions. Therefore,
in order to get sufficient work out of a man, the needs or
subsistence basis must be supplemented by a bonus upon
output or some other device for measuring productive effort.
This element of payment *pro rata* for work done is not
merely to be regarded as a necessary incentive owing to
laziness and greed. It is not merely that " I will not do
more than I am obliged to do, unless I am paid extra."
The sense of justice is curiously involved. There is a
general sentiment in favour of the view that if A turns out
more than B, he ought to be paid more, even if he ' tries '
no harder, and achieves more because he is stronger, quicker
and more skilful. Strength, quickness and skill, it is felt,
ought to be rewarded. This feeling harks back to the
individualist notion of production, which regards the immediate producers of an article as the rightful owners of that
article and of the money it will fetch in the market, dis-
regarding all social determinants of value. But it requires
recognition in a wage system, inasmuch as some payment
for output, as distinct from needs or subsistence, is in fact a
necessary incentive to industry. What a reasonable system
of payment demands is that this element shall be economically
administered. It must not be so low as to deter the stronger
or quicker worker from exerting himself as effectively as the
weaker or slower one, and so producing an output corresponding to his superiority of strength and skill. On the other
hand, it must not be so high as to give the stronger man
more than a sufficient inducement to use his strength, or to
incite the weaker to an injurious effort. A system of
' driving ' or over-stimulation, which takes too much out of
a worker, may be immediately conducive to a larger output

of wealth, but it carries a heavy bill of human cost, and lessens the use or enjoyment got out of the higher wage-payment. An equitable distribution looks not merely to the size of the pool, but to the human costs of its production and the human utility of its consumption.

The right wage-system, thus envisaged, will contain three elements, a minimum or subsistence wage, some additional payment for occupational skill, disagreeability, etc., and, where necessary, an individual differential payment. But the differential wage of occupations and of individuals tends to form a diminishing share of the total wage-bill, as better facilities of education, mobility and choice of occupation prevail.

If then there existed an arbitral or judicial body for the adjustment of wage-disputes in any trade, it would survey the particular wage-claim in this wider light, whether the claim was for a subsistence wage, or a fair wage. The effect of a wage-rise or a wage-fall in one trade upon real wages and employment in other trades could not rightly be ignored. Thus it becomes evident that, before any particular trade agreement or award can stand, it should be reviewed in the light of its effects on these other trades and upon industry as a whole. It has been the principal folly and absurdity in the recent coal settlement that, at no stage, was any reference made to the effects of the stoppage and subsequent high price of coal even upon the closely related trades of iron and steel and electricity, not to speak of the more remote but substantial effects on every other power-using trade, the domestic consumer, and so the real income of every inhabitant of the country.

If then every important dispute thus involves the entire economic system and all its component trades, it follows that any serious attempt at equitable settlement requires not merely an *ad hoc* tribunal but a standing body representative of all the interests involved in the component trades which shall be competent to express judgment upon the wider significance of the particular dispute. Such a body might conceivably have arisen from the National Industrial Council, summoned in the spring of 1919, but dismissed after the immediate danger of industrial revolution which seemed to threaten passed.

But it is not only from the standpoint of the wage-earner that some such industrial government is required. Many readers of this argument for a wage-system based primarily upon the needs of labour will have been disposed to interrupt with the quite relevant question, " What about the needs of capital ? If it is economically necessary and humanly desirable, that the wages in any business or industry shall be at least sufficient to maintain the labour in efficiency, does not the same doctrine apply to capital ? " For we are not dealing here with a communist or socialist community, but with the modifications needed to make the present industrial order tolerable. Now in this order capital, drawn mainly from private sources, is essential for production, and in order to obtain its use some payment is necessary. In other words, capital, as well as labour, requires a subsistence wage. Strictly speaking, the payment for capital that corresponds to a subsistence wage for the worker is not interest but a ' reserve ' for depreciation of plant and for business emergencies. A subsistence wage and a ' wear-and-tear ' fund would suffice to maintain the material and human fabric of a business. The wage must suffice to give ' immortality ' to the worker by enabling him, not only to keep himself alive and in working efficiency, but to enable and induce him to maintain such a family as will provide a substitute for him when he dies or becomes too old for work. But if a fresh fund of capital is required to improve or enlarge a business, or to set on foot a new business, some positive payment of interest, or dividend, is needed to evoke its use. If the business is a risky one, the payment for use of capital must be correspondingly higher. When it is said that wages is, or should be, the first charge upon the product of a business, this is not strictly true. The provision for depreciation, wear and tear, and other business contingencies, ranks on the same footing with subsistence wages, and, taking into consideration the interests of labour as a whole, the market rate of interest also stands as a necessary 'cost' of production. For, as is commonly seen, an adequate reserve for depreciation, etc., will not be maintained when shareholders continue to receive no interest upon the capital they have invested in an unprofitable business. When trade is bad and no profits are earned and no dividends paid, it does not seem unreasonable or unfair to the directors and shareholders that some reduction of wages should take place, in order to reduce costs of production. The workers, they argue, gain in rises of wages when trade is prosperous, why should they not share the loss when trade is bad? Labour has, of course, several answers, some sound, some not sound. It is not sound to urge that labour is the only real producer, and that capital, though admittedly necessary, is not productive and therefore has less right to demand some payment. Such a general indictment of the part played by capital only leads astray. Nor is it really relevant to urge that capitalists are wealthy folk, who can bear the loss of interest, whereas workers are poor and cannot bear a fall in wages. For setting aside the consideration that many 'capitalists' are poor, and dependent on the 'earnings' of capital, while many workers earn wages above subsistence rates, the bottom fact of the situation is that minimum interest is an economically necessary payment, as necessary as wages itself, if necessity admits of degrees. There is, of course, a far stronger case against accepting easily a wage-reduction, in the contention that such a wage-cut relieves the management of all motive to seek other economies in 'costs,' such as improvements in technique, in business organisation or finance. It is a valid support of demands for higher wages that in high-waged countries, like America, machine-economy, standardisation and general efficiency of management have been stimulated to the utmost. There is a fair presumption in favour of the economy of high wages, so far as the individual business is concerned. And when the wider reaction of a high-wage policy upon the volume of consumption, and consequently upon the volume of production and employment, is taken into account, the resistance of workers against reductions of wages in times of depressed trade is generally justified.

But to insist that every rise of wages will evoke new and corresponding economies in methods of production, and that these economies, reducing 'costs,' will vindicate themselves in lower prices, expanding sales and higher profits— the gospel according to Henry Ford—is manifestly foolish. There is in every trade, and every business and at every time, some limit, and a different limit, to this 'economy of high wages.' If all Mr. Ford's competitors had simultaneously adopted his policy, they could not have all met with his success, even in the most expansive of all industries. Indeed, Mr. Ford himself would not have succeeded under this condition of competition. In most industries, in almost all well-established ones, the stimulus of wage-rises to efficiency, either on the part of labour or of management, is much slighter and much slower than it is in the new and adventurous automobile industry. It is not, therefore, always possible for labour to insist before an arbitral tribunal that its demand for a rise, or even its resistance to a fall of wages, can be justified by the necessary or reasonably likely improvement in technique and management that will ensue from the adoption of its case. We must, therefore, admit that there will be some, perhaps many, cases where, owing to trade conditions outside the control of the management, the income earned by a business, or indeed a whole industry, is insufficient to pay the wage demanded by the workers, to provide a proper reserve fund, and to pay the market rate of interest on invested capital.

If labour has, as we have admitted, a claim to a subsidy towards a standard wage in such emergencies as lie outside the control or reasonable prevision of the managers of a business, so, it may be urged, has capital. Where in a naturally declining industry provision is made for displaced labour, a similar claim may apply in equity to displaced capital. Where a trust or combination finds it desirable to close down some of the factories or other plants belonging to its members, it usually compensates the owners out of the general fund. If the solidarity of interests within a single trade sustains this policy, a clear consideration of the interdependence of trades may even justify a wider policy If there is an obligation resting on the economic system as a whole to see that wages are not let down below a true subsistence point in any business or trade because of the low marketing capacity of that business or trade, a similar obligation may be valid for the maintenance of capital.

What the argument comes to is expressed in two propositions. First a true subsistence wage for labour and for capital is by right the first charge upon the income of every business. Secondly, if a business is disabled, owing to causes outside its own control or prevision, from meeting this primary obligation, this deficit should be met out of the fund of excess profits within the industry, if such fund exists, or, if not, out of the general fund of excess profits tapped by taxation and utilised in part for this subsidisation of labour and capital in weak or injured industries. The idea of a trade pool for enabling weaker businesses to pay their way is not a novelty, even where no formal trust or cartel has been organised. It is merely an application of the principle of mutual insurance inside a trade association. Its validity hinges upon the ability to discriminate between weakness or losses due to mismanagement and those due to external causes or accidents.

For wage settlements this solidarity of interests within the industry or trade is obvious  It is of prime importance to all members of a trade that no one of them shall cut wage rates, and so, by reducing costs of production, be able to undersell the rest.  Hence the adoption of a standard rate, and of trade negotiations for that standard by the whole body of employers in a trade.  But this community of interests among employers is, of course, no adequate guarantee against their agreement to keep wages low.  In proportion as an association of employers solidifies into a cartel or combine, the greater is their power for bargaining with labour, organised or ' free.'  If in point of fact wages in most trusts or combines are equal to, or even above, the standard for similar grades of workers outside, this is due either to an intelligent appreciation of ' the economy of high wages,' or to the fear of public opinion and anti-trust legislation, or to the ' liberality ' which a price-fixing combination can afford to entertain.  Where an association enjoys no such price-fixing power, it may often be disposed to utilise its strength by paying a standard rate of wages below ' fair ' or even a true subsistence level.  The recent action of the coal-owners is a case in point.

In the mining industry where at a given selling price, determined mainly from the side of demand, some mines in a district, or some districts as a whole, may be earning high profits, while others, poorer in seams or in situation or equipment, are earning low profits or none, a trade pool, by means of which a 'fair' wage for the whole trade is maintained out of a fund provided by the more prosperous mines, is the most equitable policy. Where a whole trade is temporarily depressed by causes outside its own control, there is a similar obligation on the wider fund of surplus profits and rents (or, in a word, the general revenue) to make provision for the wage-deficit. This, as we have seen, is in effect recognised, not merely in the instance of the all-administered coal subsidy, but in the whole policy of unemployment allowances and poor law relief. It is true that these public subsidies are not supposed to amount to a full subsistence wage, lest they act as a bonus upon idleness. But, as it becomes more plain that the public interest, not merely on grounds of humanity, but of far-sighted economic policy, requires that no family income shall fall below the true subsistence level, the present dole *plus* poor law allowances will have to be transformed either into a policy of public employment, or into a formally regulated system of subsidies to private industries temporarily crippled by trade depressions.

I am well aware how exceedingly alarming such a doctrine will seem to business men and politicians born and bred in the school of economic atomism and competition, where whatever anyone could legally seize in the national or world market was accounted his rightful and exclusive property. But the actual facts of modern industry sustain a totally different view of property. Put together the two facts, one, that the value of a product is determined by the play of all economic activities throughout the industrial world, and not by the activities of the individuals or groups who make that product ; secondly, that the actual apportionment of these values, thus socially created, is more and more determined, not by the adjustment of free competition, but by organised combinations, whose economic pull varies with the urgency of the public need for the commodity or service they control—bring these two salient facts into juxtaposition and our whole attitude towards individual rights of property undergoes a transformation.

Putting the result in simple language, we become aware that in such a working of our economic system, some people are getting much more than they ought to have, and others much less. We may also be prepared to accept the further proposition, that what people *ought* to have is what is necessary to sustain them in the efficient performance of any productive work they are able to do, and that what they *ought* not to have is anything in excess of this true subsistence fund.[1] This will prepare our mind for envisaging the annual product as a single socially created fund of wealth, to be divided into two parts, that which furnishes these necessary 'costs' of maintenance for the various kinds and grades of labour and of capital utilised in making wealth, and that which constitutes the net 'surplus,' remaining after these 'costs' are met. I use here the term 'net surplus' to distinguish it from the looser use of 'surplus' which I have hitherto employed. In truth both uses are justified and indeed necessary. The profits of a successful business over and above what is necessary to remunerate capital at the market rate is surplus : all rents representing the values of lands and their natural resources come within the same category : so do all payments for ability to business or professional men, in excess of what is necessary to evoke or to maintain their efficient work. All these excessive

---

[1] This use of 'ought' needs qualification. It applies here only to the human conduct and life as envisaged in the economic field. As a statement of the fuller human problem it is defective. As I show later, part of the 'surplus' 'ought' to be available for enrichment of individual life, either by communal uses or by enlargement of individual incomes, in virtue of human as distinct from economic needs.

elements of income constitute the gross surplus. But in the operation of the industrial system there are a variety of underpayments, mainly low wages, but also the 'sweating' of ability, and losses of capital due to monetary changes or other 'general' causes. These underpayments are detrimental to the good working of the economic system, they are unsatisfied 'costs,' and they should be deducted from the gross surplus in order to give us the net surplus, or fund of economic progress.

So far, I have been exclusively concerned with showing how no wage-dispute within a single business or trade can attain just settlement within the scope of that single business or trade, and how the attempt to adjudicate a 'fair' wage is found impossible unless the scope is widened to bring in that interdependence of all businesses and industries constituting the industrial system. I have provisionally applied the accepted doctrine of a minimum or subsistence wage as a rightful charge, first on the particular business, secondly on the trade, and lastly on the economic community as a whole. In this last capacity it falls upon the gross surplus, i.e. all such funds as emerge in the economic system as income in excess of 'costs.' In equity we may say that the entire body of these surpluses, rents, excess profits, monopoly earnings of ability, etc., constitute the rightful social or public income, as distinct from the proper or economically useful incomes of individuals. In strict logic, of course, the social determination of values requires us to hold that all income is 'social' in origin. But, just as we are bound to pay regard to the selfish or individual nature of every man as well as his social nature, so, in dealing with income, it is convenient to differentiate between the income that must be allocated to the individual worker, for the satisfaction of separate wants and desires, and the income which is not needed for this purpose, and to regard the latter income as peculiarly social and applicable to definitely social uses. Among these social uses, as we shall presently recognise, is the raising to a true needs or subsistence level of those wages the full charge for which cannot otherwise be met. But this is only one claim upon the gross surplus. A wider view of the functions of this surplus must first be taken. It is no exaggeration to say that the central problem of the reconstruction of industry turns upon the disposal of this gross surplus in such ways as best to promote at once the productivity of industry and the human welfare of the community. The main crux in that problem lies in the disposition of business men to separate the questions of productivity and distribution.

This business argument runs thus. The existing production of wealth is inadequate to furnish to the whole body of workers the income needed for a fully civilised life. The amount of surplus incomes of the rich, even could it be taken and distributed as extra wages, would be far too little (after allowance for the creation of fresh capital is made) to make up the deficit.[1] We must, first, get higher productivity before we can provide a satisfactory economic life for the bulk of the working classes. In order to increase productivity, the workers must lay down their antagonism towards 'capitalism,' stop their ca' canny and work harder : in bad times they must be prepared to take lower wages. It is this short-sighted doctrine whose preaching is more responsible than any other cause for the recent inflammation of class hostility in Great Britain. The upper and middle classes, disconcerted by the duration and intensity of trade depression and unemployment, are disposed to saddle the responsibility wholly, or mainly, upon the insistence of the

[1] To this proposition the support of eminent statisticians is given. See Professor Bowley's *Division of the Product of Industry* and Sir Josiah Stamp's *Wealth and Taxable Capacity*.

E

workers upon wages and hours which industry cannot bear. The workers' reply is twofold. First, in view of the growing prosperity and size of the luxury trades and the lavish expenditure of the rich, they disbelieve the employers' plea of inability to pay the current or a higher wage. This incredulity is sustained by the fact that they, or their representatives, have no access to the employers' accounts, and do not know what wages the business can afford to pay. Secondly, they argue, largely from American experience, that the necessity of paying high wages is an effective incentive to enterprise and managerial reforms on the part of the employer, and that the conservatism of British business methods leaves a large margin for reducing costs by better technique and organisation. If, whenever trade is bad, workers submit to wage-reduction, in order to enable businesses to work at a profit, this facile method of reducing costs at the workers' expense takes away the stimulus to genuinely productive economies which the pressure of circumstances would otherwise apply.

It is further argued that, in view of the revelation of excessive productive power, alike of plant and labour, exhibited by trade depressions, a reduction of wages and of workers' demands for commodities tends, instead of curing, to aggravate the trouble by still further restricting consumption in the home markets. If it be urged that a lower money-wage, reducing costs, will be reflected in lower prices for commodities, and that thus the real wages will suffer no reduction, the answer is, first, that any fall of retail prices lags far behind a fall of wages ; that, in view of combinations in the distributive trades, there is no likelihood of a full compensation by this method ; and, finally, that if there were no fall in real wages, there would be no benefit to the capitalist in profits. While the active resistance against wage-reductions is based upon the natural objection of any group of workers to reduce the price of their labour, it is supported by a wider view (shared by most social reformers outside the ranks of labour), that a progressive civilisation involves a constant rise in the people's standard of living, and that any reduction of wages, or increase of hours, is a reactionary step. Economies in production are to be sought for and obtained by a better application of the ever-growing resources of science to industry, and by a better organisation of every sort of human skill, not by wage-cuts which weaken the incentives to these true economies. There is, in the refusal of most members of the employing class to apply their minds closely to the work which properly falls within their sphere, a far more dangerous and costly form of ca' canny than any practised by workers. For the progress of civilisation depends to an increasing degree upon trained, able and enterprising thought at the top. Now the social conditions of our upper and middle-class life are unfavourable to this thought among the rulers of our business world. Education in our public schools and universities, except for an eager intellectual minority, does little to evoke, and much to repress, the type of serious thinking needed for our industrial reformation, and the young men of the employing class reared in this social atmosphere are seldom willing to apply themselves to the science and art of business with the same amount of energy, plodding industry and open-minded enterprise found in Germany and America. Sport, recreation, society, travel, unskilled politics, occupy too large a place in their life. Conversion of family businesses into Joint Stock Companies has assisted to weaken responsibility and diminish the time and serious thought put into business, at a juncture when there is an urgent call for the best efforts of industrial rulers. Though probably a very small percentage of our wage-earners have a clear perception of these deficiencies in the employing class, there is a widely diffused notion that most of the recipients of profits are 'slackers,' living a life of ease and comfort with long week-ends and other ample spells of leisure, and that Britain's lost leadership in many branches of industry is due to the refusal of the leaders to fit themselves for the conditions of the modern economic struggle.

The net effect of this working-class mentality is to confront the demand of the employers for more productivity from labour with the demand for a better distribution of the product. This seems to make an *impasse*. But it does not. For higher productivity can only be got from labour, on conditions that a larger share of the increased product goes to labour, either in higher wages and more leisure, or in improved communal services, or both. And when it is realised that, considerable as is the 'slack' of labour in many trades, the 'slack' of organisation and management is far greater, the escape from the seeming *impasse* is evident. More efficient employment of capital and labour can effect a higher productivity, provided that a due share of the proceeds goes in increased gains to the brain and manual labouring classes. It is a matter of the reasonable application of incentives. Most workers are not close economic thinkers. But experience has taught them that if, when trade seems slack, they consent to a wage-cut, competition absorbs that wage-cut in lowering prices, and that lower prices do not in fact so stimulate effective demand as to produce a recovery of trade and more employment, but produce further stoppages and more unemployment. They live in chronic fear of glutting the market. From this experience they draw the conclusion that higher productivity will be futile unless accompanied by an adequate security of increased consumption, and that increased consumption, they hold, should, and can, only come through a rise in the normal standard of income and expenditure among the workers. This conclusion is not only to them a matter of equity but of reason. For the larger demand for those standardised industrial products, where improved efficiency would operate effectively, comes from the body of the consuming public. If the bulk of the increased business incomes due to higher productivity went in higher profits, either to be spent on luxuries, or to be put back into business by process of saving, the expanding demand needed to dispose of the enlarged product would not be there. In order that full efficiency can be put into, and full productivity got out of, our staple industries, increased consuming power must be placed at the disposal of the main body of home consumers ; that is to say, the working classes. But this by no means signifies that the whole of any increased productivity belongs by right to the workers in the particular business or industry, the workers taking in higher wages part or the whole of what the employers would otherwise take in higher profits.

Here we encounter the new danger of the extension of the cartel or other combination to fresh fields of industry. I have already touched upon the growing opposition of interests between the 'sheltered' and 'exposed' trades. On the whole, the tendency in recent years has been for both profits and wages to be higher in those trades that produce exclusively for the home market than in those that produce mainly or largely for outside markets, or are exposed to the competition within this country of imported goods. This has meant that sheltered trades, producing goods or services of an indispensable or important nature, have been able, partly by express agreements, partly by tacit consent, to maintain prices at a level yielding a surplus above subsistence payment for capital and labour, in a normally well-equipped and well-managed business. That is to say, they have by higher prices taken for themselves a larger share of the total national product than upon any fair assessment of effort, skill, or ability, they are entitled to.

Now cartelisation, and in general the movement towards organisation of trades in trusts or combines, has no express connection with 'sheltered trades.' Though in a few instances a sheltered trade, e.g. building, has in its supplies of materials been blackmailed by price-fixing combinations, the trust and cartel movements both in this country, the Continent and America, have generally originated and developed in industries connected with products such as oil, steel, machines, chemicals, textiles, sugar, which figure in the world markets. The displacement of free competition by combination has been brought about by a favourable conjunction of various factors, preferential access to natural resources, or to transport facilities, governmental aids by tariff or subsidy, advantages of large-scale enterprise in technique, organisation of markets and finance, operating to keep the bulk of the industry in a few large companies with the alternatives of profitable combination and cut-throat competition continually before them. Except in the case of sheltered industries, the power of trusts or combinations to control prices in Great Britain has been limited by our policy of free imports. But even before the war the efficacy of this safeguard was challenged in certain important trades by the extension of the trust or the cartel into international trade. The Committee on Commercial and Industrial Policy after the War [1] thus reported the pre-war situation :

" British combinations and firms have in a number of instances been parties to international agreements for the delimitation of markets and the regulation of prices. A well-known case is that of the International Rail Syndicate, and other examples relate to such diverse commodities as

[1] Cd. 9053, 1918.

wire-netting, aniline oil and sulphur black, and some other chemical products, glass bottles, tobacco and certain non-ferrous metals."

After the war, this new form of international capitalism is pursuing a more vigorous career. The deliberate policy in Germany with governmental backing, for the organisation of all the leading industries into national cartels, has had a considerable effect, as an example, upon industries here and in other countries called upon, either to fight these cartels in the world market, or to come to terms with them by forming similar national organisations. The revival of the Steel Cartel on the Continent is a first-fruit of this movement, and the coal situation in this country has evoked serious proposals for enabling the British industry by a common selling agency to come to some agreement with other coal-producing countries for an agreed mobilisation of output and regulation of prices. In a number of great industries, endowed by modern technique and power with a potential productivity far outrunning their visible market, such arrangements are the only escape from cut-throat competition, violently fluctuating prices, unreliable employment and immense wastes of capital. In many business quarters where before the war combinations on a national scale were looked at askance, there is a growing disposition to give serious consideration to them, and, in industries catering for world markets, to entertain proposals for safeguarding home markets and come to international agreements fo the distribution of neutral markets.

Now our immediate interest in these organisations lies in their bearing upon industrial peace, and the need for some conscious elements of industrial government. Whether we regard organisation in the 'sheltered' trades, with a view to the maintenance of prices designed to secure higher profits and wages for their capital and labour than are attainable in the exposed trades, or the organisation of national cartels as units in a wider international cartel, we are confronted with a conflict of economic interests wider and in some ways acuter than that between the capital and labour in the several trades. For these strongly organised trades are not merely in a position to secure large economies, by better regulation of production and elimination of the wastes of competition, but by their control of prices they can over-charge other industries dependent on their products and the consuming public in general, distributing this 'loot' among the members of their close corporation. Though discretion may lead the cartel magnates to pacify their employees by wages and other conditions above the outside level, they will naturally tend to fix their prices at ' what the trade will bear ' and the consumer must pay. Where the cartel or combine virtually controls the whole trade in an essential industry the price will generally be very high. Where there exist some considerable independent firms capable of cutting, instead of following, the cartel prices, or where the article is not indispensable, or some substitute is available, the cartel will raise prices less, may even lower them. But the conflict of interests between strong trades and weak trades will become keener and more formidable, if the movement towards combinations upon a national and an international scale proceeds.

There are, indeed, two influences upon which some rely to cancel or to mitigate this conflict. Let these trusts and cartels come out into the open, it is argued, let them be required to give full publicity to their finance, public opinion will then act as a sufficient deterrent against abuses of their price-fixing power. Others rely upon the 'change of heart' which they think takes place in great monopolist corporations, the magnitude and intricacy of whose operations makes the directorate

management virtually independent of the effective interference of greedy shareholders. Such big businesses are in
reality public services, and their rulers come to be affected
by this sense of public service, alike in their relations to
their employees and to the consumer.

But this is too romantic a psychology to be convincing.
No doubt publicity may do something to hold avarice in
check, but it will only prove effective if some power of
public coercion stands in the background. Nor can we
see the dominant nature of the successful modern business
man—hard, able, self-assertive, adventurous, accustomed to
have his own way and impose his will upon his underlings,
suffering the process of conversion from profiteer into
voluntary servant of the community.

Trusts, cartels and price-agreements among sheltered
trades will mean a constant tendency for these strong trades
to make excessive gains at the expense of weaker trades.
Nor is this merely a conflict of interests among capitalists.
Whether the excessive gains of the strong trades be shared
with labour in high wage-rates, bonus shares and other
benefits, or not, the injury inflicted by high prices on the real
wages of all other workers carries the conflict into the ranks
of labour and complicates the issue of industrial peace.

Consciously, or unconsciously, every form of industrial
conflict, between capital and labour in a particular industry
or business, between sheltered and unsheltered, combined
and competitive trades, between skilled and unskilled,
organised or unorganised labour, turns eventually upon
claims upon the surplus wealth which modern methods of
production turn out in excess of what is economically
necessary to sustain the capital and labour employed in
production. There may continue to be disputes in industries
as to the precise measure of a true subsistence wage for labour
or for capital, but it is to the interest of both parties that

subsistence wages shall be paid. It would not pay the workers in a cotton mill or an ironworks to press a demand for higher wages which could only be met by reducing the subsistence rate on capital, any more than it would pay the employers to force wages down below the efficiency rate for labour. In freely competitive trade, as we have seen, wages and profits tend to be kept at this subsistence level, though improvements in the arts of industry may cause temporary surpluses divisible according to the economic strength of the two parties. But the salient feature of the present economic situation, the formation of strong industrial combinations, gives rise to large lasting discords for which our industrial system provides no settlement. Sheltered or combined industries are able to fix prices which, after paying all economic costs, leave large surpluses which, whether due to economies of organisation within the combined industry, or to high prices imposed upon the market, represent a fund of wealth to which the combination has no equitable claim. Economic peace cannot be attained by piecemeal references of particular disputes of capital and labour in single businesses or trades. For such a course ignores the interdependence of businesses in a trade, and of trades in the industrial system. This interdependence, as we see, affects at every turn the rates of wages and of profits that can be paid out of the sale of the product of any business. The modern movement towards combination, placing in the hands of a group of strong trades a power to take for their own gain an increasing share of the improvements of industrial methods, lifts the whole question of peace in industry from the plain of detailed settlement by groups of employers and workers in single businesses or trades to the higher level of a general equitable distribution of the ' surplus ' representing social advancement in the arts of industry.

# IV

## COSTS AND SURPLUS

W**e** are now in a position to reset our problem of industrial peace in terms which indicate the wider steps that must be taken.

Since the wages and profits payable in any business depend only in part upon the efficiency of its management and labour and the size of its product, but mainly upon the productivity of other industries, i.e. upon the working of the whole industrial system, producing goods which exchange in larger or smaller quantities against the product of any single industry, no labour dispute can in equity or in practice find a satisfactory settlement within the confines of the single business or industry where it has arisen. For both the causes of the trouble and the effects of any settlement will in large part lie outside the business or trade.

This view is summarised in a treatment of industry as a single complex organism, producing a fund of wealth, divisible into two parts, one required for the wages and profit which sustain the life and current activity of the organism, the other a surplus, over and above these costs of maintenance, a fund of social and individual progress.

There will remain some difficulties in measuring these costs of maintenance, which, as we have already indicated, are not fixed and uniform amounts, either in the case of wages or profits. The chief difficulties which arise in respect of 'fair' or 'efficiency' wages we have already discussed. The varying physical and psychical conditions attaching to different sorts of manual and mental labour involve rates of payment, in order to evoke and maintain the output of productive energy. We also recognise that the 'costs' of the application and maintenance of capital and business enterprise will widely differ in different businesses. At any given time and place there is, indeed, a fairly standardised price at which capital and efficient managerial ability are procurable for a secure business use. Here we have a fairly calculable bill of 'costs' on the side of capital. But in the business world there are widely divergent elements of risk which must be provided for in the rates for capital. And there is another still more refractory element. There are types of rare business ability—inventive, creative or organising—so serviceable in the ways they utilise the capital and labour at their disposal that they appear to be able by a few strokes of genius, or by abnormal periods of concentrated thought, to multiply manyfold the output of a business. As the result of a few new mechanical inventions, some improved factory organisation, the discovery of some valuable by-product, some skilful stroke of marketing, a rapid expansion of productivity, income and profits may accrue. The typical business judgment, ascribing the sole causality of this 'surplus' gain to the business genius, insists that the whole of it belongs to him by right. He has made it himself, and it is his individual property. The further statement is made that any interference with this personal reward for ability will cause this high productivity to be withheld, and society at large will be the loser, because the ultimate gains of these great economic advances come to the consuming public in better or more plentiful goods at cheaper prices. Now, on the question of sole causation we will not linger long. Though most successful inventions and improvements are built upon many past experiments, and represent the final step in a process to which many others have contributed, the person who first makes the process available in a business sense has certainly some claim upon the surplus of which his action was the efficient cause. But there is no equitable ground for asserting that he should have the whole. For, however important his contribution is, it is not the sole determinant of the surplus. The technical ability and business genius of Henry Ford would not have made his millions, had not the conjuncture of demand in the United States, based upon the various activities of innumerable past and present Americans, co-operated with the formation of his business and rendered it so profitable. There is no way of separating and measuring the value of his separate contribution. How much is it socially desirable that he should have? Not the whole, a whole the size of which he could not possibly have contemplated and desired. No. If it could be intelligently ordered, Mr. Ford should have as his share just that which would have sufficed as an inducement to do as he did. Most great inventors have got very little, their inventions passing cheaply into the hands of business men with just the intelligence to realise their worth and the necessary capital to exploit it. The work of creation in all the arts is in large measure its own reward, in the sense that the interest, and perhaps the personal prestige, of the achievement are the chief incentives to the work. In a less measure this is also applicable to the more distinctively business operations that expand productivity or transform productive operations. Business men, engaged in these great operations, will doubtless count upon handsome rewards, and the hope of such rewards may be necessary to evoke their full efficiency. Such rewards may thus reasonably rank as costs of production in our scheme. It will pay society to see that such prizes as appear to be necessary incentives to certain types of business ability shall be secured to them. But this is no reason for identifying these payments with the whole of the surplus gains that emerge in such operations.

Would not Mr. Henry Ford, Mr. J. D. Rockefeller or any other multi-millionaire of modern industry have done what they did for one-half, one-quarter or probably a much smaller fraction of the fortunes they have reaped ? Because it is not possible to estimate closely the payments which would in such cases furnish a sufficient incentive, that is no reason for assuming that any interference with these huge surpluses is dangerous.

When, as is commonly the case (especially where the monopoly, or quasi-monopoly of powerful combines enters into the profit-making power), the conditions that make large profits possible are rooted in the purchasing power of the community, it is wanton waste to leave the bulk of these great business gains to be piled up in huge personal fortunes. The net effect of such excessive payments is not to sustain, but usually to weaken, the efficiency of the recipients. For, whereas a reasonably large gain may be a partial, or a chief, inducement to many business men to devote their time and energy to skilful improvements, a plethora of unexpected gain will tend to demoralise by its sheer irrationality, or will lead to premature retirement in pursuit of other interests.

The net result of this argument is to indicate that, while considerable prizes may fairly be accounted ' costs of production ' in the more adventurous branches of industry, in these cases as in others, where gains are got by organised squeezing of consumers, a large ' net surplus ' emerges in various parts of the industrial system.

Let us now return to our main distinction between costs and surplus. There is, as we perceive, no true discrepancy of interests in regard to the portion of those proceeds of a business which are entitled to rank as costs of labour, capital or ability. With full publicity of accounts, it ought usually to be possible for representatives of labour and capital sitting round a table with a reasonable amount of intelligence and good will to reach an agreement in such matters of misunderstanding as will from time to time arise. But, where a business or an industry finds itself by force or luck in possession of a ' surplus,' there is no possible basis of rational agreement for its apportionment among the owners and the workers. For it is not produced by, nor does it belong to, either of these parties. In other words, it is part of a socially created fund, attached by force of bargaining or price-fixing to the income of particular businesses. It is only by thus realising the economic surplus as a social fund that seekers after industrial peace can move towards their goal. For almost all conflicts between employers and workers in the several trades and industries, and between the stronger and weaker trades and groups of trades, are attempts, direct or indirect, to secure some portion of this surplus. Industrial peace can only be secured by removing this surplus from the arena of strife and seeing that it is administered for the general welfare.

In order to give meaning to this policy, it is first desirable to envisage clearly the services which the surplus is required to render. And here it is necessary to distinguish the true net surplus which accrues when full provision has been made out of the industrial product for the subsistence costs of all the capital and labour that is employed, from that larger surplus which is swollen by the gains that strong economic groups or trades are able to obtain at the expense of weak ones by driving the latter below the true subsistence point.

The net surplus has three functions to perform : (1) it must cover the savings needed for the enlargement and improvement of the industrial system, so as to make provision for a growing population or a rising standard of consumption in the future ; (2) it must furnish the public revenue by means of which government is able to carry out all its non-remunerative services ; (3) subsidies, or other aids, which may from time to time be required to redress the damage done to the subsistence fund of any vital industry, by causes of a political nature, or otherwise lying outside the possibility of adequate provision by the industry itself, must be provided out of this surplus. Upon the gross economic surplus will fall the obligation to redress the damage done to the subsistence fund of a weak trade by the forcible pressure or control, exercised by a stronger trade upon which it depends for some important material or instrument of production.

Now none of these essential tasks can be performed without a more consciously considered public policy than has hitherto existed. No consideration has hitherto been given to the size and direction of the flow of savings socially useful and desirable for the enlargement and improvement of the capital fabric. Though it must be obvious to any reflecting mind that, having regard to the arts of production and consumption in a community, and the probable growth of population, there must be at any given time a right proportion between saving and spending, economists have almost universally assumed that the larger the proportion of the surplus that is saved the better. Never have the advantages of an enlargement and improvement of the public services, to be furnished out of this same surplus by diverting it into public revenue, been set against the advantage of leaving it to accrue as private capital. The assumption has always been that national expenditure should be kept low, in order that as much as possible of the surplus may take shape in new privately owned capital. This is no doubt largely due to the persistent delusion that the 'surplus' is created by, and is the rightful property of, those who receive it as income, instead of being a body of wealth due to social conditions and activities. Taxation for public revenue should, therefore, be kept at a minimum. But as soon as the nature of the surplus as a socially created fund is grasped, the belief in the advantage of unlimited saving should disappear. The folly of the belief is transparent to students of the actual business world, when the failure of public and private consumption (save in periods of war or other emergencies) to keep pace with the increasing power of capitalist production has become a commonplace. The recurrent periods of trade depression, or under-production, are a fatal register of the futility of attempts of the saving members of our industrial society to create new capital at a faster rate than it is, or can be, used. Why should it be regarded as likely that the unconcerted action of innumerable private persons or business firms should put into the industrial system the right amount of new capital, or should distribute it among the different industries in the right proportions? Even if all investors were fully apprised of the relative values of all investments, and were free to put their savings to the best advantage—the now false assumption of an obsolete *laissez-faire* system—this method would be very wasteful. For the check of falling interest is notoriously slow and imperfect as a deterrent to over-saving. As matters stand to-day, there is no guarantee that either the total amount of saving, or the proportions of its investment, concur with the real needs of industry.

Moreover, as governmental services swell in size and importance, the amount of capital expenditure made by the State assumes a more considerable part in the total economy of saving, and must be expected to reduce the proportion of the surplus available for individual or company savings. The larger quantity of surplus taken by taxation, and applied either to capital or current expenditure on hygiene, education and other useful work, does not, of course, necessarily signify an actual diminution or depletion of the private saving fund. For, if a large part of the public income is expended in ways which give greater security of

F

livelihood, and raise the standard of physique and intelligence of all classes, improved efficiency of brain and manual labour may be expected to express themselves in higher economic productivity. Thus, in face of the increasing claims upon the surplus for public purposes, the growth of that surplus may be so fast that the saving fund available for capital investment may be increased rather than diminished, and may even form a larger proportion of the total income, assuming that the advancing structure of capitalism calls for a larger unit of capital *per capita* of labour. The actual rate of saving will, however, no doubt in the long run be affected by the disposition of government to take for current public services an increasing proportion of the surplus, while at the same time taking over, or controlling, those great fundamental industries which are passing into trusts, cartels or other price-fixing combinations. In other words, the great business corporations, which under present circumstances do the greater part of saving for industrial development by means of large reserves, will find their ability to handle these great increases of capital considerably curtailed. A larger proportion of the saving fund will represent the choice of investments by individual savers, or the financial institutions which assist them. One of the most urgent practical reforms in the business world consists in the collection and publication of reliable financial statistics for this process of investment, and the elimination of the reckless or planned misinformation which causes so large a proportion of savings to be lost in enterprises only profitable to those who organise or float them.

The claim for some measure of public supervision and direction of the flow of new capital is urged to-day by financial economists, who, like Mr. J. M. Keynes, hold that industrial development is a national and not merely an individual concern, and that high dividends are not always a true index to the national utility of investments. Nobody would desire to revert to the war-time restrictions upon investment, and the preference given to the Empire over foreign countries in respect of trustee investments has little to commend it, for the development of wheat lands in Argentina is at least as valuable for Britain as the opening of diamond fields in South Africa. Such public supervision as might be exercised should be directed to securing full understanding of the social utility of investments, rather than to prohibition or even definite selections. An impartially constructed body of financial experts could do great service in such an advisory capacity, exposing rotten companies and checking other wastes of the saving fund. But no coercion is desirable in the direction of private capital. Industrial progress demands that individual investors shall adventure capital in risky or experimental undertakings, in which large losses are frequently the necessary costs of ultimate success. The planners of a fully socialist community would, of course, be required to scrutinise more closely the social value of each application of new capital. But the structural alterations of our system, needed for industrial peace, do not carry us so far. While public control will be exercised for two main purposes, viz. the security of subsistence costs of labour and capital, and a general direction of the uses of 'the surplus,' the large amount of industry remaining in private enterprise will continue to require to be fed with fresh flows of capital directed by the adventurous sagacity of individual investors or their expert advisers.

Taxation for purposes of public revenue, national or local, tends everywhere to take a larger amount of 'the surplus.' The association of taxation with 'the surplus' is direct and intimate. For though taxes may be levied in such a way as to encroach, temporarily at any rate, upon subsistence costs, properly speaking, such incomes have no ability to bear a tax, and any attempt to extort it is an error of judgment damaging in its reactions upon trade, and in the last resort upon the taxable body of wealth. There is always a tendency for taxes, however imposed, to shift from elements of income with no ability to bear, i.e. subsistence wages or minimum interest, on to elements of 'surplus,' i.e. incomes which are not economically necessary to induce their recipients to apply the factor of production in virtue of which they are received. As a tax on agricultural products, or on houses, tends to settle upon economic rents (a form of surplus), so a tax imposed upon, or shifting on to, abnormal profits, dividends or salaries, is borne without injurious reactions upon industry. This, as we have seen, is a strong unrecognised testimony to the social origin of surplus, the fact that it can be attached without affecting individual incentives.

But acceptance of the principle that taxation tends to lie upon different elements of 'surplus' does not dispense with the exercise of skill in the art of taxing, so as to cause the least disturbance to 'costs.' Some waste, or other injury, is always caused, when the incidence of a tax or rate is shifted from the income of the payee on to some other party, often by some concealed and intricate movement of prices. This is the condemnation of almost all taxes upon commodities or economic activities, such as purchases, or transfers of property. Only in countries where direct taxation is difficult to assess or to collect can a case be made for indirect taxation. With the group of fallacies that support protective tariffs I cannot here affect to deal. It must suffice to say that economists are in pretty general agreement that there are four main methods of tapping the economic surplus : (1) so far as economic rents of land can be measured and assessed as distinct from 'improvements,' they form a suitable subject for a specific tax ; (2) an excess profits tax, levied on a basis of several years' returns of net profits was found of serviceable yield during the war and the post-war boom, and will be a necessary permanent instrument of revenue if, as is likely, large private enterprises pass more and more from competition into combinations with price controls ; (3) a graduated income tax, with super-tax, will probably remain the chief instrument of revenue, though the assumption that the larger the income the greater the pro-portion of ' surplus ' it contains is not in all instances correct. But though there are cases where a rising income tax may deter a man from putting out the effort to earn the income, or may cause him to spend income which he would have saved and invested (thus securing future dividends on which taxes would be paid), the extreme difficulty attending exact measurements of surplus renders this rough-and-ready instru-ment of taxation exceedingly productive of revenue which, could it be analysed, would be found mainly to consist of economic surplus. (4) Inheritance duties may be regarded as the best available method of securing for society a large share of those high gains of ability, initiative and enterprise, which it is found advisable to leave as prizes to successful busi-ness men under the play of the capitalist system, partly because they are necessary incentives to the output of personal skill and energy, partly because it is easier to assess them in the lump at death than as passing elements of annual income. The obvious social disability of allowing great wealth to pass by inheritance, with the immunity of personal work which it conveys upon recipients who had done nothing to earn it, is winning an ever-growing approval for limitations of inheritance which a generation ago would have been deemed an intolerable interference with the sacred rights of bequeathal.

But while the State as the instrument of taxation has an indefinitely great claim upon the surplus on behalf of the public services, it by no means follows that the administration and expenditure of all this 'public' revenue should be conducted by the political government. That would be to ascribe an absolutism to the State, in relation to other social institutions, that is highly questionable. A good deal of the suspicion directed against the 'interference' of government with business, and much of the resentment against high taxation, are due to a conviction, often well-founded, that a government of politicians, and of politically appointed bureaucrats, has not the qualities for the efficient, economical and successful conduct of business. It is true that the larger concern of modern governments with business matters tends to modify the old conception of politics, and we have to-day significant appeals to the electorate for 'a business government.' But the older political atmosphere still prevails, and those who, for other reasons, oppose the nationalisation even of essentially monopolistic industries such as railways, electric supply and banking, or even the closer control of such industries by the Board of Trade, base their opposition on the alleged incompetence of official management. A part of this mismanagement, it is argued, comes from the extravagance of public undertakings, due to a 'recklessness' in the expenditure of the taxpayers' or ratepayers' money from a yielding to improper political pressure for high salaries and wages, and for the allotment of lucrative contracts. A certain slackness is imputed to all public employees, and 'the government stroke' has become a byword. It is often replied that the test of a comparison with private profitmaking enterprises is invalid. Public enterprises are not out for profit; it is up to them to set an example in good pay, short hours and other conditions of labour, and, if necessary, to supply goods or services below cost price, making up the deficit by revenue derived from other remunerative services, or in the last resort from taxes or rates.

But this is not a wholly satisfactory reply to the charge of official inefficiency, and the preference for a business management, as far as possible independent of politics, has strong support by no means confined to the ' capitalist class.' If it is desirable to nationalise the railways or banking, by means of public acquisition conducted by the State, that is no reason for leaving these important businesses under centralised State management. Modern socialism rather signifies a group of virtually self-governing industries, in the operation of which all the active interests, viz. managerial ability, the various grades of employees, consuming industries and the private consumer, shall be duly represented, with the State as a final controller in matters of finance. Though this form of public service is nowhere fully worked out, recent experiments, especially in Germany, and to a less extent in some other countries, tend in this direction.

The underlying principle of the whole of our argument favours this practical solution. Industrial peace, we argued, is impracticable by confining the settlement of a dispute in a particular trade to the employers and workers in that trade, without taking due account of the interests of labour and capital in other trades, and in the general consuming public, affected by the dispute and the terms of settlement. In other words, the vital principle of the interdependence of trades, carrying with it a social determination of all values of goods and services, must enter into any satisfactory government of an industry. Conflicts and stoppages and wastes are due to the false envisaging of a business or an industry as an independent self-sufficing entity, paying what it must to, and taking what it can from, other outside businesses, but having no organic relations towards them. Our interpretation of the industrial product as an integral whole—a social income, part of which should be utilised in several business forms as costs of maintenance, part as surplus, available for industrial and other social benefits—receives clear corroboration in the present attitude towards public services. Revenue derived from income endued with 'ability to pay' is applied to the gratis supply of many public needs and utilities, national and local, and is available for the partial support of other services for which specific payments are made by their beneficiaries. That a particular branch of postal service, or a particular tram route, or indeed a total tram service, does not pay its own costs, is not deemed a conclusive reason for dropping a service which may have great personal or social utility. Such a policy of subsidies may be involved in the best expenditure of the general revenue. It is an application of the principle of distribution according to needs, which, wherever it can be applied without any weakening of incentives in the persons or services subsidised, carries an increased yield of human welfare.

The utilisation of public revenue for the extension of communal services is a policy with an intimate bearing upon industrial peace. For the pressure of the workers towards a higher standard of life, which is a chief source of industrial conflict, may be met to an increasing extent by provisions that lie outside the wage system. A brighter town or village life, with a variety of free opportunities for education, recreation and enjoyment, with cheap theatres and concerts, sports grounds, dance-halls and other amenities, might go far towards breaking down the barriers that have separated the leisure and the pleasure of the classes from those of the masses. I stress this aspect of communal services, not because it is either humanly or economically of such great importance as the services of hygiene and sanitation and insurance, but because its supply of vivid personal interests and enjoyments contributes more directly to the consciousness of sharing in the progress of civilisation.

How far it is desirable that communal services should subsidise wages, directly, as in the instance of free meals for school children, cheapened housing, etc., may best be treated as belonging to the economy of emergencies. But the utilisation of public revenue for family allowances is a direct assertion of the related principles of social determination of value and distribution according to needs. It is economically defensible upon the ground that a portion of the socially created 'surplus' can and should be applied to equalise the standard of living among the larger and smaller families of the workers. By placing, as it does, the welfare of children in the foreground, the proposal is the strongest challenge yet uttered to the inequity, inhumanity and waste in the current operation of our wage system. No single extension of our communal expenditure would go so far to redress the general sense of the defects of that system, or to add to the sense of family security required to disarm the wasteful irritability of class strife. It has to meet two present difficulties due to short-sighted selfishness. The first is the large new immediate demand upon the revenue it would involve, with a failure to perceive how the better distribution of income and expenditure would react in stimuli both to personal efficiency, enlarged consumption and higher productivity. The second is the reluctance of labour to admit that some reduction in the basic wage and money income of unmarried or childless workers in certain trades might reasonably be accepted, in view of the far greater benefits accruing from the policy to the workers as a whole. For there is no ground for supposing that so large an addition to public expenditure as any adequate scheme of family allowances would involve could be raised out of immediately available 'surplus,' without some contribution from those members of the working class whose wages already stand well above subsistence rate owing to freedom from family ties and obligations. In this brief treatment of family allowances I am assuming that the provision is made communally, not by separate industrial funds. For the latter involves the acceptance of the supposition that each trade must always stand on its own financial feet, and is, or should be, able to meet all socially desirable demands out of its separate funds—a supposition seen to be fallacious.

Upon the third use of the 'surplus,' viz. the temporary aid given to an industry injured by some political action or by some outside event beyond possible prevision, there is no need for me to dwell here. Such provisions should always be in the nature of emergencies. For if there were an industry which was vital to the community, but which could not be conducted so as to pay its way—the possible situation of our railways in the near future—that industry should be taken over and run as a public service. If the 'dye' industry were, as it is not, one that it were vital to maintain within our national system, the same policy would apply—nationalisation, not subsidy.

But, it may be asked, if this 'surplus' is to be employed so largely upon the three purposes of, first, furnishing the saving fund, secondly, extending communal services, and thirdly, providing emergency subsidies to damaged vital industries, no provision appears to be made for raising the real wages, shortening the hours or otherwise improving the remuneration of the workers. Is their only gain to be attained through communal expenditure, with such reactions upon standard of living as may be attained through family allowances ? The nature of my answer to this question has already been intimated in my brief discussion of the problem of saving. Every movement of economic policy in the direction of distribution according to needs, whether accomplished by organised labour pressure, or by larger public services, will signify, not only a fuller utilisation of wealth, in the sense of enlarged human welfare, but a stimulation of productivity. For the needs economy implies a more regular and certain pressure of consumption upon production, and thus not only takes in all the 'slack' apparent in the present working of the industrial system, but furnishes a constant incentive to improvements in the arts of production, by banishing that panic fear of overproduction which is to-day the chief deterrent of progress.

Now, though we have envisaged the real income of the community as divisible at any time into two funds, a subsistence fund for capital and labour, and a surplus, to be utilised in the ways we have described, this does not imply that either of these funds is a fixed amount. As the level of civilisation rises, the private as well as the communal requirements of men rise with it, and a larger amount, though not necessarily a larger proportion, of the increasing product of industry must be applied to 'subsistence' and 'fair' wages. For the liberty of man requires a certain personal margin over and above physiological or conventional needs, and the full subsistence of an alert and educated worker with many interests in life demands a variety of satisfactions and experiences, involving ampler leisure and personal expenditure than the ignorant and torpid-minded worker of the past.

It is here that the double urge of the population question becomes manifest. A freely proliferating working class, offering a rapid easy supply of cheap labour, weakens every incentive to industrial progress in the employing class : they will not exert themselves to invent or utilise better machinery or other labour-saving economies, so long as workers are plentiful and cheap. An expanding population thus keeps wages near the physiological subsistence point, because, on the one hand, the supply of labour is large, on the other, because employers, devoid of stimulus to progress in the arts of industry, cannot afford high wages. Thus there is a close and genuine harmony between birth-control, industrial progress and a rising standard of life. If we ask what is the 'optimum' population for a given country in a particular stage of economic development, no exact answer seems possible. For much depends upon the value we set upon life as such. But most thoughtful persons will agree that a limited population, with a secure and sufficient economic basis, continually evolving new and higher needs which they are able to satisfy, is worth a good deal more than an unlimited population living shorter, harder, duller and more precarious lives. Civilisation not merely depends upon, but consists in, the substitution of quality for quantity of life. The demand for a higher standard of living everywhere forces to the front of conscious policy this problem of population. It is, indeed, at present one of the chief bulwarks of nationalism. Each advanced country fears the free immigration of prolific outsiders, on the one hand, and the competition of the imported products of cheap foreign labour on the other. The support given to legislative measures for restriction of immigration and for protective tariffs by workers in most high-wage countries is attributable to these fears. To the wider implication of this international conflict we will revert later. At present it remains only to note that workers are everywhere becoming alive to these direct and indirect implications of the population question as bearing upon their demands for a higher standard of life. Its special bearing upon the subject of family allowances deserves a word. Critics of that proposal not unnaturally lay stress upon the influence it may exert to promote earlier and more numerous marriages, larger families, lower child mortality, so unduly feeding the labour market and impeding industrial progress through cheap labour. The offhand reply that the proposed allowances cannot be conceived as adequate inducements to have large families does not satisfy. At present the fear of the expense of another child is undoubtedly, among all but the most ignorant and reckless grades of workers, an actual restraint, and this restraint would be removed or greatly weakened for low-paid labour by any such allowance. More convincing is the argument that family allowances, taken in conjunction with other social provisions for imparting security of liveli-hood to all grades of workers, will tend to bring the unskilled workers, hitherto the more prolific, nearer to the level of maintenance, education and responsibility attained by skilled workers who have already taken on birth-control as a family policy. That the policy has been moving down-wards fairly rapidly from the middle to the skilled working classes is statistically proved, and the recent advances of lower grades of labour in wages and organisation make it pretty certain that their birth-rate will also be affected. But it would, I think, be foolish to deny that, for some time at any rate, a family allowance without restrictions might serve to retard the otherwise desirable rate of decline in births, and that it would certainly lower the rate of child mortality. A policy expressly directed to secure a better distribution according to needs ought certainly to safeguard the higher standard of life it is intended to promote, by recognising the inherent inconsistency between this higher standard and an increasing population. In other words, the family allowance policy must be guided by some plain recognition of an ' optimum ' population. If it is estimated, for example, that an average birth-rate of three is sufficient to secure or maintain the ' optimum,' the child allowance should not be extended, say, beyond the fourth birth, taking into consideration the families which will in any case be childless or contain fewer than the ' average.'

An unrestricted birth-rate was compatible with considerable general economic progress at a time when this country held so strong a leadership in the arts of mechanical production as to be able to purchase all the foreign foods and raw materials she needed by the profitable sale of increasing quantities of her manufactures. Some rise in the general standard of living was then consistent with a very wide disparity of incomes. But now that we cannot any longer count upon a large and constant expansion of our foreign trade, and our workers are restive under the failure to continue the nineteenth-century progress in their wages and other conditions, the safety of society and the efficient working of our industrial system become dependent upon a rigorous limitation of the population of this country. Without hesitation, it might be affirmed that such control is an essential condition of industrial peace, inasmuch as without it there can be no considerable surplus for communal and individual expenditure, and no security for full subsistence wages with regular employment.

# V

## A PEACE POLICY FOR INDUSTRY

OUR main argument has been directed to show that no trade dispute can obtain a reasonable and satisfactory settlement, either by force or voluntary agreement, without involving the more or less important interests of other trades and the general consuming public. This follows from the very nature of industry as an organic whole. In other words, whatever mode of settlement of such a trade dispute is adopted, adequate opportunity must be afforded for the effective representation of these wider economic interests. The large view here taken of subsistence fund and surplus, as the products of the activities of the whole industrial system, will by some be interpreted as a concession of the full case of socialism. Only a completely socialised society, it will be said, can secure industrial peace with justice. If the time has come for some conscious government of industry to displace that unconscious regulation of competing interests which no longer works, that conscious government must either be State socialism or some self-government of industry as a whole with an independent status of its own. Either the State must permanently take charge of the entire industry of the country, as it began to do in the temporary emergency of the war, or it must abdicate the economic functions it exercises now (with the exception of some limited taxing power) and hand them over to an independent representative economic government. But the rigour of such logic collapses before the criticism of the practical judgment. Nobody with business experience would seriously maintain that our present State, furnished with a more elaborate officialdom, could conduct successfully the operation of the industrial system with all its interrelated branches, or that our parliamentary system, fortified perhaps with a section or chamber of industrial representatives, could exercise an effective popular control over so vast a tangle of political and economic institutions and activities as would fall within its province. The known weakness both of bureaucracy and democracy would find exaggerated expression in such State socialism. Indeed, recent experiences of democracy in countries where its formal sway has been most fully established do not dispose even the severest critics of ' the capitalist system ' to entertain any firm belief that the popular franchise could become a competent instrument for the control of a State entrusted with the economic government.

On the other hand, it is equally impossible to envisage the satisfactory working of an industrial government, independent of the political State, or merely related to it by the obligation to pay taxes for its support. It would be impracticable for the State to divest itself of any of the main controls over, and contacts with, industry it exercises now, and fulfil the essential functions of a political government. A brief reference to the nature of these controls and contacts makes this manifest. Apart from the use of the taxing powers, the State intervenes in (1) the maintenance of public order and the enforcement of contractual obligations ; (2) the legal regulation of railways, mines, factories, workshops and other businesses, in the interests of employees, consumers and the general public ; (3) the issue of legal currency ; (4) private legislation for the compulsory acquisition of land and other property rights by ' public utility ' companies ; (5) the ownership and operation by the central or local government of certain business undertakings, such as public education, the postal, telegraphic and telephone services, some banking and insurance, and the various municipal businesses for the supply of streets, light, transport, water and amenities of local life ; (6) interference with housing and other functions coming under public health. To these specific contacts of politics with economic activities may be added a general obligation for the maintenance of 'essential services,' implied under the primary conception of the function of a State to defend life and property. It is, indeed, a reasonable doubt as to the ability of the State to perform successfully this last obligation, that has brought many minds to the recognition of the necessity of drastic reforms in the government of industry. For the maintenance of 'essential services' is the acid test, and the knowledge that its failure would bring not only industrial but political collapse, demands not a weakening but a strengthening of the relations between industry and the State.

But such a judgment does not signify any movement either towards wholesale State socialism or a more rigorous exercise of central bureaucratic powers in those spheres of activity above enumerated. On the contrary, the claim put forward in some quarters for the active participation of advisory councils, in which skilled representatives of the interests of labour and of consumers should take part in the operation of the public services, is of vital importance not only for the invigoration of these services but for the education of a more expert criticism in a public otherwise a plastic material for interested manipulation.[1] But the association of groups of workers, business men and citizen-consumers, with the administration of public functions, finds an increased importance when we contemplate the strengthened and enlarged control which the State must

[1] Cf. Laski, *A Grammar of Politics*, for a comprehensive statement of this proposal.

G

exercise in the interests of that measure of industrial government required for the security of industrial peace.

In the new industrial order the State must assume a different attitude towards three types of industry.

(1) When effective competition is inherently impossible or impracticable, while at the same time the services are of literally vital importance to the community, the alternatives presented being public or private monopoly, public ownership of the industry or service is necessary. Whether such monopolies shall be administered directly by public officials, or shall be 'farmed out' to 'companies' under rigorous conditions as to conditions of employment, rates and qualities of services, is a matter not of principle but of expediency. Indeed, it would in some measure be a field for experiment. Though, for example, it may be generally agreed that the main branches of the transport trade by land and electric supply should not only be owned but operated by the State, there is something to be said in favour of leaving banking and insurance to be operated by companies under public direction and regulation. But since the issue of money is a primary function of the State, and the principal form of modern money is bank credit, it is evident that State control over the general conditions of the issue of credit must be established. Whether this condition is consistent with the continued existence of joint-stock and private banking belongs to the general problem of the competence of the State in the exercise of business controls. And this may remain a matter for experiment. In any case the State will have the right and obligation of drawing from these monopolies such surpluses as, within its price-fixing discretion, it may allow them to levy from consumers of their products.

(2) While the presumption may be in favour of State ownership and public operation of essential monopolies in transport, power, money and insurance, the relation of

government towards trusts, cartels and other combinations in important, though not vital, industries demands closer consideration. The widespread and rapid tendency of some staple and many subsidiary industries into some form of output-restricting and price-fixing combination presents a delicate problem. As we have seen, these price-fixing practices are definitely hostile to the interests alike of other industries and the consumer, while the surpluses they take at the expense of both are injurious to the peace and progress of industrial communities. What can be done ? It is equally difficult to stop these combinations being formed, and to break them up when formed, as much American experience attests. The State and industrial society must either live with them or absorb them into public industries. Now it may be said at once that there is no general support from public opinion in this country, still less in America, for a general policy of the nationalisation of trusts and cartels. There are minor policies for dealing with certain distributors' combines, as in the coal and milk trades, by public agencies, that command wide approval. But though the movement towards combinations has made considerable advance since the remarkable disclosures of the Trusts Committee in 1918, there is no belief in responsible quarters that the State could advantageously buy out and work any of these quasi-monopolies. This is partly because few of these handle 'necessaries,' partly because, as a rule, their control of the market is not complete (real or possible competitors surviving), partly because many of them fluctuate in strength, and sometimes dwindle and expire, partly because they are secret in their operations of control.

Indeed, the current attitude, both of the business world and of the general public, towards mergers or combines, actual or contemplated, in the chemical, metal or textile trades, is surprisingly favourable. This is attributable largely to the magic of the word 'organisation.' Germany and America are, it is widely held, out-competing us in many world markets by their superior technical or financial organisation. We must meet them with their own weapons. Our businesses must stop fighting one another for raw materials and contracts, and present a united front to the enemy. This involves combined action on an agreed plan, of which limitation and specialisation of output, common selling agencies and distribution of markets are chief essentials, unless the closer form of a trust or single holding company be preferred. This presentation of a national strategy for fighting the foreigner in our home and neutral markets serves to mask the serious dangers to our own industries and consumers which the movement contains. For, as we have already indicated, the notion that public opinion, or any sense of public service on the part of the business men who run combines, will adequately safeguard the public against the tyranny of price-fixing and profiteering is quite chimerical. The Imperial Chemical Industries merger in its very share structure anticipates the profits which its virtual monopoly will enable it to win. The price of tobacco, sewing-cotton, cement, imported meats, salt and a large variety of articles, controlled at some stage in production or distribution by combines, contains larger or smaller elements of monopoly profit, according to the elasticity of demand in each case. So far as the net profits of these businesses are placed on record, they put beyond doubt the exercise of this oppressive power, though in many instances watering of capital, hidden reserves and other financial devices of concealment prevent the public from realising the extent to which they are robbed. If, as we have supposed, the State is not at present qualified to take over and to operate the increasing number of industries which practise these arts of combination, varying from 'gentlemen's agreements' to complete mergers, it must at any rate develop some effective safeguards against the related abuses of capitalistic ca' canny, or restriction of output, and a price-fixing policy directed to take 'all that the trade will bear.' At present no policy has been thought out beyond the useful word 'publicity.' Yet even that word suggests that industries of this condition must be regarded as quasi-public bodies with definite obligations to the other industries and bodies of consumers whose welfare depends upon getting adequate supplies of the controlled products upon 'fair conditions.' There is, we have already observed, no ground for believing that publicity of accounts, with such disclosure of profits, reserves, etc., as can be enforced, would furnish a sufficient safeguard for fair prices. Whether the State could intervene successfully, by regulation of prices, would greatly depend upon the nature of the industry and the variety of its product. Where a single, fairly standardised article, such as cement, salt or milk was produced or distributed by a combine or trust, it might be possible to apply a 'gas-clause,' regulating profits on a sliding scale with prices. But when we turn to such industries as steel, or chemicals, or even soap, where a large and ever-changing variety of products and by-products is concerned, it is difficult to believe that a governmental price-control could be exercised by such a sliding scale or any method of cost-taking. Power might usefully be given to a Trust Department of the Board of Trade to intervene where some flagitious instance of price-raising was reported, but a continuous process of cost-taking, essential to a checking of the prices of a large number of products constantly changing in composition and methods of production, would not be practicable. To assail by legal prohibition cartel agreements for restrictions of output by quota arrangements may at first sight seem feasible. But, if applied with rigour, it would drive the cartel members into the closer structure of a merger which would be free to regulate its output according to its own will. Nor would it seem reasonable to try to force the members of a cartel to work full time, or to operate its weaker plants, when there was seen to be no adequate demand for its products. It would not be easy to prove that in any given case the motive for restriction was the raising of prices to consumers.

Probably a judicious use of the taxing power would be a more effective instrument. A highly graduated tax on excess profits would at any rate divert to public revenue a considerable part of monopoly profits, and might even be applied so as to remove or abate restrictions upon output.

(3) In trades where the interests of the consumers are safeguarded by effective competition, and where supernormal profits can only be earned by unusual business capacity, or in boom periods, the intervention of the State will be confined to securing subsistence wages and other minimum conditions for labour, emergency subsidies where trades are temporarily damaged by causes outside their control or prevision, and to providing equitable tribunals for settlement of disputes between employers and workers. New enterprises in an early non-competitive stage of development should have a free run for their money, subject only to minimum conditions of employment and other factory regulations. If better general control of industry, credit and prices could be secured, the greater regularity and security of ordinary manufacturing businesses would tend to place them on a changed financial footing. Debenture or fixed interest shares would supply the necessary capital, and the removal of even the appearance of profiteering would go far towards creating an atmosphere for industrial peace.

Summing up this argument, the State's part in the new government of industry would be to assist in securing a subsistence wage for labour and capital, to remove, either by preventive methods or taxation, those surplus profits which are the bone of contention between capital and labour, or between stronger or weaker trades, to utilise them for social services and for emergency aids to industry, and to provide pacific modes of settlement for such disputes as might continue to arise.

Conflicts will continue to arise, partly from ignorance and misunderstanding, partly from genuine divergences of interest in the distribution of emerging surpluses. But we have seen that none of these conflicts in businesses or industries can be settled 'on their own merits,' because they have no separate merits.  An unsettled dispute, ripening into a strike or lock-out, vitally affects other trades and the consuming public : but so does a settlement involving some rise in 'costs' and prices.  If the 'other trades' and the consumers have an interest in any specific trade dispute, they should have a *locus standi* in its settlement.  Now that many trades are bound together alike on the side of capital and labour, by national federations, this solidarity of interests finds conscious expression.  An attempt in any one industry to raise or lower wages or other conditions is realised at once as a policy which both directly and by imitation will spread to other industries.  Thus an atmosphere favourable to some wider organic mode of settlement of trade disputes has already been prepared.

In the turmoil which immediately supervened upon the end of war, the Government took a sound step in the right direction by setting up a National Industrial Conference, with representatives of capital and labour from the principal trades, and with an element of disinterested experts.  The committees of this Conference began with recommendations of standard wages, hours and other conditions of employment when, the immediate danger past, the whole experiment was dropped. Yet here we had the nucleus of an advisory self-government for industry, which, had it been permitted to live, might have grown into the very instrument needed for working out and administering the principles of industrial peace. The establishment of a permanent National Industrial Council in which capital, labour, the consumer and the government should be duly represented, a body endowed at first with purely advisory powers, is the first essential of that limited industrial self-government needed to secure industrial peace. Such a body could not, of course, confine its activities to considerations of trade disputes; it must also develop policies of constructive co-operation, not only between capital and labour, but between trade and trade, gradually building up the necessary fabric of that conscious government which we have seen is needed to replace the unconscious government of a competitive system that is passing away.

It is no part of my purpose here to do more than indicate the general lines of such a project. It should be directed to perform upon a wider national scale the work which the Whitley Councils, the Trade Boards and the Industrial Court in their several ways were designed to do. The failure of the first to fulfil in any adequate way the purposes of their founders, the grave difficulties of the Trade Boards in raising conditions in the weaker trades to a satisfactory level and the incomplete structure and insufficient powers of the Industrial Court are alike due to the attempts to solve piecemeal a problem which is not susceptible of such a treatment. That each trade best understands the troubles that are its 'own,' and that its representatives should co-operate for their consideration, is no doubt true. But its chief troubles are not exclusively its own, and they can only be overcome by a wider consideration and a more general treatment. The national solidarity of industrial interests demands an instrument far more representative in character and far more pliable in method than the controls exercised by Government Departments. The Committees of this permanent National Industrial Council should be in a position to give authoritative advice not merely to the industries but to the government, so far as legislative or executive authority is needed to give effect to their advice. And a chief immediate function for the Council would be to establish provisional standards of remuneration, hours and other conditions, for various grades and classes of employees, having regard to the nature of their work, the needs of their families, and the normal capacity of the trade to bear the costs of these conditions. Such standards would furnish the rules which suitable arbitration tribunals would administer in cases of dispute referred to them when the preliminary processes of conciliation and negotiation between the parties had failed to reach a settlement. The arbitrators on these tribunals should be competent persons drawn from a panel, and should take into consideration, not merely the claims of the two parties directly concerned in the dispute, but those of outside trades and consumers affected by any settlement involving supplies or prices. On the arbitration tribunal also would be conferred the right of recommending a subsidy to meet the case where the trade, owing to causes outside its control, was unable temporarily to meet the terms of the award out of its own resources. The appointment of the panel of arbitrators might be partly by Trade Unions and Employers' Associations, partly by election by the Whitley Councils, Conciliation or Trade Boards representing the several trades, partly by governmental appointment, partly by nomination by locally elected bodies whose interests would be those of the consuming public.

In our earlier analysis we pointed out that serious industrial conflicts were not confined within single trades, but that the struggle between stronger and weaker, sheltered and exposed, trades was assuming increased importance. Indeed, the disputes over wages between capital and labour in the several trades are in large measure derivations of this wider discord. For in the strong trades they are attempts of the workers to get their share of surplus gains : in the weaker ones they are protests against 'sweating,' which in large measure is the misfortune, not the fault, of a weak trade with no surplus and often with a price-level below the true subsistence point for its labour and capital. This situation would be relieved to a considerable extent by the measures here proposed. For the taxation of excess profits would reduce the strength of the strong trades, while the use of this surplus by the community for communal services and for subsidies would level up the condition of the workers in the weak trades.

But there still remains one issue of vital importance. Though the inability of many weak trades to meet the claims of labour for 'fair' conditions, and for some share of the rise in the general productivity of industry, is partly due to the ability of strong trades to take an excessive share by price control in a restricted market, this is not the only source of their weakness. In export trades, exposed to the active and growing competition of goods produced abroad by means of cheap labour, and sometimes cheap materials and power, the rates of wages and of profits are to some extent determined by those prevailing in the competing countries. For 'the economy of high wages and short hours' has no absolute validity. In countries where the workers are inured to hard conditions, sweating may 'pay' in low grades of production. It is beyond question that some important branches of our export trades are driven to the alternative of paying low wages, or going out of business, on account of the growing competition they meet in foreign markets they once held, and on account of the invasion of their home market by cheaper foreign products.

There are four possible ways of dealing with this situation. One is the *laissez-faire* solution of allowing our trades to cut down wages and hours to the level of outside competitors. That may be ruled out at once as hostile to our accepted standards of civilised society. The second is to let trades or sections of trades, that find themselves unable to live without sweating, die out, and to assist the displaced labour to flow into other occupations which can and do conform to civilised conditions. This sounds excellent as an economic theory, but it is met by grave difficulties in practice. Where the inability to pay decent wages is due to 'bad times,' it is very difficult to find any alternative employment for displaced labour, and a large public expense, with damage to the morale of displaced workers, is incurred by keeping them in idleness. Moreover, when trade revives, some of these weak trades may find themselves thriving and able to meet all reasonable claims of labour. Here is where the case either for a subsidy, or for a protective tariff, has its most specious appeal. These trades, it is contended, can pay their way quite well, even with foreign competition at home and abroad, except in periods of general depression or some exceptional damage to their sources of raw materials or their normal markets.[1]    But, though a tariff might do good to such trades in their home market, that benefit would be less during a general depression and fall of purchasing power than when times were good, while it would injure them in foreign markets by reason of the keener competition of foreign goods excluded from our

[1] It cannot, however, be assumed that a trade thus exposed to the fluctuations of the world market is in a position to make adequate provision out of its profits in good times against periods of deep and protracted depression.

market. Sound social policy might, indeed, support a subsidy, if the goods thus produced, by preventing unemployment or short time, could find a market without a further lowering of prices and a consequent demand for increased subsidies. But where the inability to pay fair wages is due to 'bad times,' and not to some exceptional misfortune of the particular trade, the case for a subsidy collapses.

The situation of weak export trades brings up a basic fact of the industrial system which I have so far purposely ignored, viz. the fact that our industrial system is in some important aspects international, and that this condition renders it impossible to get a complete establishment of industrial peace by purely national modes of settlement. So long as the size of our population and the small proportion of our home-grown foods and raw materials keep us so largely dependent for our living upon our exports of manufactured goods, we cannot hope to improve the standard of living for the mass of our workers without something like a corresponding rise in the standard of life in foreign countries that produce what we buy and buy what we produce. The attempt to raise our standards, as if we were a self-dependent economic system, would simply drive out of business our weaker trades, or if they were sustained by subsidies derived from taxation of stronger trades, would drive new savings to invest themselves abroad where higher dividends were attainable and the taxation of which could be more easily evaded. In the last resort such a policy would lead to the de-nationalisation and domicile abroad of an increasing number of our richest people. But even if this increased export of capital could be prevented by governmental intervention or discriminative taxation, the root of the trouble would remain. If the manufactured goods, which must be sold abroad to pay for our necessary foods and raw materials, could not find a sufficient market at prices that would cover their 'costs,' our other trades would be starved of their raw materials and foods would be scarce and dear. In other words, the real income available for distribution would not suffice to raise, or to maintain, the civilised standard of living for our whole population. Emigration of our workers to our Dominions and to foreign countries with relatively high standards of life would take place to an increasing extent, if the policy of these countries permitted. But at present the tendency both in our Dominions and in the United States is to welcome our capital but to look askance at any large migration of the sorts of labour we can spare. The dependence of our national economy upon the world economy is so close that our wage-problems cannot be solved completely by a purely national mode of settlement. Nor can any reasonably likely development of imperial resources help us in this matter. There is no early prospect of so large a growth of population in and exportable supplies from the Empire as to make us independent of foreign supplies. In every decade there are one or two years when the export supply of wheat from the wheat-growing members of that Empire simultaneously fails, and we are thrown on foreign supplies for the first necessity of life. The same applies to many other articles of prime importance to our trade and life. The slight increase in the proportion of our import trade from the Empire since 1913 affords no encouragement to the notion that we can greatly lessen our dependence upon foreign supplies. Nor do statistics bear out the widespread belief that our Empire is taking an increasing proportion of our exports. The preference the Dominions give us counts for little, in view of the efforts of each Dominion to promote by tariffs and subsidies its own manufacturing industries.

In any event, the development of our Empire is not likely to contribute any more to the possibility of raising standards in this country than the development of foreign countries. For the expansion of our export trades in the near future, Russia, China and South America offer far greater possibilities than any portion of our Empire.

The prime essential for the security and progress of our export trades is international co-operation. The work initiated before the war for international agreements on conditions of employment has already been extended by the activities of the International Labour Office and the Economic Section of the League of Nations. The full scope of this work for a sound international economy has, however, hardly begun to be comprehended. The standardisation of minimum conditions of employment in the advanced industrial nations in hygiene and hours requires to be supplemented by some agreement between members of the League regarding wages, not necessarily aiming at uniformity of money or real wages, but at reasonable security for nations with higher standards against the competition of foreign sweated labour.

There is, indeed, a wider aspect of this problem which the League has hardly yet professed to take into account, viz. the possibility of co-operant capitalism in the advanced nations using the coloured populations of Asia and Africa as semi-servile instruments for the cheap abundant supply of raw materials for their mills and foods for their workers. An economic inter-imperialism of this order appears to be emerging in the capitalist finance that aims at developing the backward countries in the tropics and elsewhere. If the League gains some of the strength and prestige of an inter-national government, the weaker outside peoples of the earth and the lands they occupy may easily, by an extension of the Mandate policy, become its subjects. Whether the spirit of League policy would be sufficiently humane and equitable to apply effectively the principles of a trust for civilisation which its Covenant lays down, in face of the demands of a capitalism so influential in its constituent national governments, remains an open question. But whether or not the definitely international machinery of the League were thus extended to the interests of the ruling industrial nations, the large and increasing part of the world which has passed or is passing under the control of a few Western nations as colonies, protectorates, mandates, spheres of influence, concessions and the like, may easily become a huge 'sweating system,' by means of which national and international capitalism may make larger profits out of cheaper labour than they can or dare employ at home. Portions of the rich resources of these newly developed countries may be used to raise real wages and other conditions in white men's countries at the expense of the backward peoples. This is not a mere fancy, it is what in some measure is happening, not, however, as part of any conscious concerted policy but as the loose outcome of the play of economic forces in a rapidly expanding internationalism.

How difficult it is to prevent such a policy of exploitation is illustrated by recent disclosures in Kenya, and by the difficulties which the Mandate Commission of the League has encountered in its dealings with the Mandatory Powers. In such happenings we get glimpses of an economic conflict wider than those to which our attention has mainly been diverted, a struggle of the stronger peoples to fasten an economic domination upon the weaker, so that by concealed modes of 'forced labour' and unequal bargains, they may get large surplus gains to be distributed, mainly in dividends at home, but, partly, also in concessions of conditions to white labour that may serve to produce quiescence and connivance with this new phase of inter-imperial capitalism.

Such an exploitation of the backward peoples, whether conducted by national or international groups of capitalists, is in accordance with traditional practices, and, though challenged by the more humanitarian spirit of our day, has generally prevailed. In the long run, as I have already indicated, it is an economically unsound policy. For the full utilisation of the modern arts of production in the staple export industries demands a continuously and rapidly expanding market for those factory products which these industries produce, and that implies a wide development of standards of material comfort and of purchasing power in the populations of these backward countries. In a freely competitive system this socially advantageous economy would prevail. But if the future of the great export trades, iron and steel, textiles, chemicals, etc., passes into the shape of national or international cartels, this security for maximum production and consumption, as we have already indicated, disappears. For the finance of cartels and trusts, aiming at maximum net profits for their shareholders, commonly requires a restriction upon output that cramps the technical efficiency and productivity of industry.

Thus in this widest setting of industrial conflict, as in the narrower conflicts of capital and labour in the several national industries and of the stronger and weaker national trades, the struggle is between surplus profits with limited production and maximum production with equitable distribution of the product. How far and how fast it is possible for the economic instrument of the League of Nations to gain from its constituent governments an adequate recognition of the supreme importance of a conscious policy of economic regulation of the treatment of backward peoples and the resources of their countries, in the interests of a true world economy, it is difficult to predict. The problem in its full and conscious shape is so new, the political instrument for handling it so imperfect, public attention is so absorbed in narrower issues, that the success of competing economic imperialisms, or of an inter-imperialism, as the less dangerous alternative, may seem assured. But as the lesson of the dependence of political world-peace upon the satisfactory adjustment of the relations between the economic interests of advanced and backward peoples is more thoroughly learned, there is reasonable hope that a policy of sound economic internationalism, based upon equality of access to the resources of backward countries, and a fair treatment of their peoples with a view to the education and supply of their constantly expanding needs, may gain enough authority to break up the new and subtler forms of servitude devised to replace the crude slavery of the past.

"But," it may be urged, "if the validity of all your schemes for industrial peace hinge upon the early success of this sound international economic policy, the outlook for a nation like Britain so dependent upon foreign trade, is indeed a dismal one. For, whereas in all advanced industrial countries strong central and local governments exist, capable of bringing into operation those schemes of equitable settlement of trade disputes, and of the fair disposal of 'surpluses' here proposed, the establishment of an international government with comparable powers for handling world economic problems seems a far distant possibility." But, in reply, two things may be said. First, even in those countries most dependent upon foreign trade, the peaceful settlement of most disputes can be achieved by the methods of national mediation and arbitration, accompanied by a proper system of taxation and social utilisation of 'surpluses.' Secondly, the rapid growth of internationalism in banking and investment, international cartels, concessions and consortia, is certain to obtrude with great frequency and persistence into League politics, bringing home with great urgency the need for strengthening the economic authority of League instruments for dealing with the rela-

H

tions of capital and labour in the international field. If the organised forces of national and international capital are not to capture, hold and operate, the League for the new capitalism, without regard either to the workers who elect the national governments that constitute the League, or to the interests of the subject peoples outside the League, the urgent need for international economic government must find expression in actual world policy. This view does not premise the setting up of an elaborate central world-control, but rather of an economic federalism in which the application of certain common accepted principles and policies shall be undertaken by the national governments—an extension of the restricted covenants already entered for particular economic objects, such as limitation of the hours of labour, prohibition of night-work for women, etc. How fast the obstacles to the formation of these binding national agreements can be removed, and a genuinely international spirit can be introduced into the sphere of world industry, is a matter for experiment and prayer. It is perhaps the most fundamental of all the issues involved in the attempt to extend to its full limits the great idea of a self-governing community. For the early progress of this idea much depends upon the outcome of the conflict already visible in the operation of the League, between the representative democratic principle incorporated in the Assembly and the principle of forcible oligarchy enthroned in the Council.

Ignorance and selfishness are here as elsewhere the enemies of human progress. In the international field the selfishness of little groups of hard-headed business men, who know what they want and mean to get it, is too often consecrated as patriotism and nationalism. The exposure of this sham can only be achieved by revelation of the actual facts and forces in world trade and finance. To this great educative task the Economic Section of the League, in co-operation with the Labour Office and the Mandates Commission, should devote itself with indefatigable zeal. Already we have in the Institute of Agriculture a working instrument for the collection, standardisation and publication of agricultural information throughout the world. Many branches of industry, commerce, transport, finance, are privately organised, both nationally and internationally, through trade organisations and Chambers of Commerce, for information and for conference. The League's economic sections might make it their chief business to co-ordinate the information derived from these and other official or non-official sources (including the immense number of Trade Journals) so as to make available as complete a picture as possible of the actual state and movements of the world economy. Absence of this easy access to reliable information is a chief cause of the bewilderment which blinds both individuals, peoples and their governments, to their community of interests and the co-operative policies by which this community may best be realised. Light is the first need for the education of an international mind and morale.

*     *     *     *     *

In bringing my argument to its close, I find one state of mind with which I must briefly deal. It may be called 'the impatience with machinery.' "You propose," it will be said, "to solve problems of conflict, in which the passions, interests and misunderstandings of men are engaged, by endowing governments with new and various powers of intervention and control, and by setting up Committees and Tribunals and Commissions with elaborate powers and regulations. But our economic processes are already over-regulated. What is really wanted is not more machinery, but 'a change of heart,' of which there are already many signs, if it is allowed free play and is not stifled by laws and regulations imposed from outside." And it is true that we have well-meaning employers and politicians who tell us, in *The Times* and elsewhere, that employers and workers alike are prepared for 'a square deal' and that 'a spirit of co-operation' between capital and labour is only waiting for a call. This, of course, is no new language. It dates far back in the throes of the Industrial Revolution, it inspired the appeals of Carlyle, Ruskin and the Christian Socialists ; it belongs to the social philosophy of the Charity Organisation Society, which finds the solution of all social problems in individual character and conduct. Now while there is a sense in which it is true to say that the only beings capable of conduct are individuals, and that all sound conduct is derived from personal character, this is no valid plea for holding that social problems can be solved by leaving them to unorganised individual will and action. A social problem requires a social solution, in the sense that there must be common consciousness and agreed co-operative action in dealing with it. But this co-operative action demands laws, institutions, organs of common conduct. The term ' machinery,' though sometimes convenient, is a dangerous misnomer for expressing these organs of co-operation. Improperly constituted, or abused, they may, indeed, harden into the similitude of machines. But rightly formed and employed, they are not ' machines,' or even ' organs,' but modes of spiritual co-operation, exceeding far in their freedom and creative energy any of these lower instruments. The distinction here is of vital importance. Machines do not educate, they only evoke a forced conformity to fixed mechanical conditions : organs in their form and capacities respond but slowly and with difficulty to the needs of their constituent cells. But a legislature, a committee, a corporation, if it is really inspired by a common will, idea or purpose, continually affects its individual members and makers, and reciprocally is affected by them.   Thus the habit of working together in some regularly constituted body acquires, by this interaction of whole and parts, an accumulative rate of progress : it works better, because the intelligence and will of its individual members improve, and these in their turn improve, because the committee, tribunal, commission, works better.[1]

It is idle to trust to ' common sense ' or 'a sound heart ' in order to obtain ' a square deal ' when the cards are packed against you.   A genuinely common sense must find expression through such modes of common consultation and action as we have been investigating, ranging from National and International Governments down to works committees, if it is to be effective for industrial peace.

In conclusion, it may be well to draw more closely together the threads of my argument.   No pacific settlement of a trade dispute, involving wages or other costs, can be satisfactory which does not take into consideration the reactions of the settlement upon other trades and the consumer. For the notion that a trade dispute is a matter to be decided by the parties to the dispute alone, whether by the test of force, involving a stoppage of work, or by agreement between the parties, ignores the essential interdependence of industries in the economic system.   The stoppage in a particular trade, or a rise or fall of wages, or other costs of production, in that trade, must in greater or less degree affect the interests, perhaps the very life, of other trades. Every action of the employers or workers in a fundamental trade, such as coal or transport, affecting the price of the product, *ipso facto* affects the real wages of all workers and the real incomes of all other members of the community. Yet there exists no provision for bringing this solidarity of

[1] Cf. Miss Follett's *Creative Experience* for a full setting of this important thesis.

interests to bear, either in preventing a dispute, or in arranging satisfactory terms of settlement. This obstinate separatism of attitude is largely due to a failure to recognise that the capital and labour employed in any business or trade are not the chief determinants of the value of the goods or services which they produce. That value is jointly determined by what goes on in that particular trade, and in all the other trades from which the demand for the product of the particular trade proceeds. This central fact of the social determination of value involves a flat denial of the claim of labour or capital in a business to the takings of the business on the ground that they have made it. The social determination of all values should in reason and in equity be accompanied by their social distribution. This would signify a distribution according to maximum utility of consumption, i.e. according to needs. But wealth, instead of being distributed according to needs, is distributed according to the economic strength of the respective claimants. Every process of bargaining or price-fixing is a test of economic force between the buyers and the sellers. Each party gets something, but, except in the rare instance of an exact balance of power, one party gets more than the other. If free competition and equality of opportunity prevailed, such a distribution might be moderately satisfactory. But in the actual play of modern industry, natural or organised scarcity, on one side or the other, signifies that distribution takes place by ' pulls ' and ' squeezes,' the weaker bargainer getting little, the stronger much.

From this inequality of bargaining, by which landowners, capitalists, men of business and professional ability or skill, extract heavy payments, there emerges a body of ' surplus income,' over and above the sums for which the owners of scarce factors of production would consent to sell their use, if they were unable to get more. So far as subsistence wages and minimum payments for capital and ability are concerned, industrial harmony exists. But over the seizure of the 'surplus,' as most of it appears in rents and profits, conflicts are waged, not only between capital and labour, but between stronger and weaker trades, and between groups of trades and financiers in different countries for the exploitation of new markets and backward countries. The extenuation, sometimes offered, that the 'surplus' only forms a small proportion of the whole body of wealth, ignores the fact that its bad distribution is the direct cause of the under-consumption which even in normal times keeps industry functioning below its strength and is responsible mainly for the enormous wastage of trade depressions. Much of the labour unrest to-day is due to a half-conscious perception that the economic system is worked wastefully, and that better distribution is the key to higher productivity.

Industrial peace can then only be attained in proportion as this actual and potential surplus, the fund of social progress, is put to its best uses. A completely socialist community might seem to be demanded for realising the related theories of social determination of value and distribution according to needs. But neither the politics nor the economics of any Western nations seems adaptable to ideal socialism or communism. Everywhere there are intractable elements that must be conciliated. No one favours an all-powerful State, or can devise a system of completely self-governing Industry that would work. We are, therefore, thrown back upon partial remedies and indirect approaches to industrial peace. Some inequalities can only be slowly removed, some surplus gains must be conceded to personal greed and power.

But a double line of advance to peace can be plotted out. The use of the taxing power, in order to claim large portions of the surplus for genuinely communal services, would at once abate the acerbity of conflict and promote a needs distribution. The provision of equitable tribunals for the settlement of disputes, so constituted as to command the confidence of the parties directly concerned in the dispute, while at the same time giving due consideration to other interests substantially affected by the issue, would furnish an alternative to settlement by force that would have on its side the growing weight of civilised public opinion.

This statement still leaves one doubt unsolved. Will workers and employers in all cases consent to abandon the 'right' to strike or lock-out, accepting instead the method of conciliation or arbitration? Will they insert in all labour contracts an 'all in' arbitration clause, and will they undertake to stand by the award? Here we come to a definitely moral test. The 'right' to strike or lock-out is only valid as a right of self-defence, so long as no better remedy is available. This right is always defective in two ways: first, in that no man can be a just judge in his own cause; secondly, in that it involves risks or injuries to others who are not parties to the quarrel. It would appear, then, that the right to stop work disappears when the alternative of equitable arbitration is presented. "But," it will be urged, "does not this involve an unwarranted and an unenforceable interference with the liberty of the subject?" 'Unwarranted,' because the vendor and purchaser of any goods or services must be permitted to refuse to sell or buy if the proposed terms of purchase are unacceptable. 'Unenforceable,' because workers dissatisfied with the wages or other terms of employment cannot be compelled to work, while employers who hold that their business cannot bear the proposed wages cannot be compelled to pay them. The first objection, however, disappears when the full significance of a business as a social function is realised. The workers or employers in an industry are not warranted in creating a stoppage which blocks the whole thoroughfare of industry, and deprives the consuming public of some necessity or convenience of life, because they insist upon a price higher than that which equitable arbitration has awarded. The right of refusal to sell or buy except on terms satisfactory to the bargainer is conceded for ordinary conditions of marketing. But society always reserves the right of intervening when a monopoly or scarcity, natural or contrived, threatens public order or vital interests. This social right must always override the individual power to fix a price, for a price is a thing with a social import : it affects not only the two parties directly bargaining, but others. An equitable tribunal has, therefore, the right to overrule a price, even though the two parties may have agreed on it, if it be held injuriously to affect other parties.

The other objection, the practical difficulty of compulsion, is graver. There are here two distinguishable issues, that of compelling the parties to a dispute to put it to arbitration, and that of compelling them to accept the award. Three compelling influences are available. First, the sense of reason and equity in the disputants, educated and fortified by the clearer understanding of their social obligations, and by the knowledge that they will get 'a fair deal.' Secondly, the influence of outside public opinion favouring a pacific settlement and expecting it. No strike or lock-out could hope for success with no outside assistance or good will. Thirdly, comes the possibility of legal coercion. In principle a strong case can be made for total prohibition of organised strikes or lock-outs as breaches of public order and injuries to otherwise defenceless third parties. A completely socialist community could not permit any group of workers to refuse to do their share towards the social unkeep, on the plea that they were more competent to decide their pay and hours than the government. They would work on the terms laid down for them, or starve.   But in the improvised modicum of industrial government envisaged here, milder measures would, I think, be desirable and would suffice. Contracting parties should bind themselves under pecuniary penalties to have resort to arbitration and to await an award, but should be free to refuse the award and to cease work afterwards.   But no assistance out of any public funds should be available for those refusing an award to an acceptance of which they were pledged in the terms of their contract, and if their dependents became public charges, relief should be given under such conditions as prevented it affording support to the recusants.   In the possible case of employers maintaining the necessity of closing down their works, because they could not bear the increased labour costs involved by an award, a case would lie for application for a temporary subsidy from the portion of the social surplus allocated to this purpose. It might, however, be desirable to allow alike to employers and employed an appeal from the Arbitration Tribunal to a Court charged with the duty of determining whether the award of the former body trenched upon the subsistence fund of labour or capital in the industry concerned.

It will be said by some that all these arrangements and provisions will not make men work, or employers keep open, on terms which do not satisfy them.   The answer is, " Perhaps not if they think, or feel, that they can do better for themselves by taking the matter into their own hands and using such economic force as they can muster."   There will perhaps always be those who will insist on using force to get all they can, without regard to others.   But the changes here proposed, for enabling them to get something like their fair share of what is going by pacific and reasonable methods, will prevail among the generality of men, and an ever-growing power of public opinion, directed against the folly, waste and wrong which conflicts involve that are

' fought out to a finish,' will reduce such scandals to the negligible position that duels occupy to-day in the annals of most civilised communities. If, however, this view of industrial educability is too sanguine, it does not diminish the importance of removing certain obstacles to understanding and good will, and of offering improvements in the methods of industrial peace.

This more peaceful and productive economy will prevail in proportion as employers and workers come to realise that industry in its essence is not a fixed mechanical structure, but a human activity, created and controlled by the co-operative wills and intelligences of men. The industrial conflicts of the recent past will then be regarded, not as lasting oppositions of power and interest, imposed by the very nature of industry, but as temporary maladjustments that can be resolved by a better understanding of industry as a continuously creative process, striving to make new business structures, adapted to the demands of an age when technical changes of vast importance require for their full utilisation the active consent of all the agents of production, based upon a fair participation in the fruits of industry.

Printed and bound by CPI Group (UK) Ltd, Croydon, CR0 4YY
08/05/2025
01864551-0001